ENDORSEMENTS

"Like a fine surveyor, Kerry McRoberts helps the reader navigate Montgomery's thought with care and consideration, treasuring the artifacts and evidence left behind by one of Christendom's leading thinkers of the 20th Century."

— Brian Nixon, D.Phil.
Veritas International University.

"Kerry McRoberts' work captures both the unique impact of John Warwick Montgomery as the leader of the "legal-evidential" school of apologetics for over 50 years, as well as Montgomery's uncanny ability to be at front stage in about every battle over the reliability of the biblical text and over Jesus Christ as the center of that reliable text. Montgomery insisted on first being known as a lawyer (American attorney, English Barrister and French Avocat, to boot!) and only then known as a theologian, philosopher, and historian. This book explains why the church Militant is fortunate he insisted on that priority!"

— Craig Parton, J.D., M.A.
Trial Lawyer, Santa Barbara, CA., and Director of the International Academy of Apologetics and Human Rights, Strasbourg, France.

"John W. Montgomery educated an entire generation of students of the Bible and a host of apologists with his insightful legal-historical defense of the faith. Dr. Kerry McRoberts has done a masterful job in penning *Faith Founded on Fact* which honors Dr. Montgomery's lifetime of service! Dr. McRoberts's thorough and thoughtful chapters that interact with Dr. Montgomery's thoughts on various important subjects does a great service to readers who seek interaction with Dr. Montgomery's ideas. I highly recommend this unique and respectful work!"

— Joseph M. Holden, PhD
President, Veritas International University.

"John Warwick Montgomery was a giant in Evangelical apologetics. A learned historian, theologian, and lawyer — and a faithful Lutheran minister — Montgomery influenced generations of Christian thinkers. Although we did not share the same confessional tradition — I am Catholic — or philosophical inclinations — I am a Thomist — I count myself blessed to have studied under Professor Montgomery in the early 1980s prior to my going off to doctoral studies at Fordham University. In this accessible and readable book, Dr. McRoberts introduces the reader to Professor Montgomery's apologetic method and how he applied it to the question of Christian truth. Even if one finds oneself not entirely in agreement with McRoberts or Montgomery — as I have on occasion — there is much to learn from this highly influential and important way of defending the Christian faith."

— **Francis J. Beckwith, PhD.**
Professor of Philosophy, and Church-State Studies,
and Associate Director of Graduate Studies in Philosophy, Baylor University.

"John Warwick Montgomery was one of the greatest defenders of the faith for the past sixty years. He was a prolific author, a successful lawyer, theologian, historian, and a brilliant thinker. But, like most brilliant thinkers, his thought was very profound and often complex. This is where the author, Dr. Kerry McRoberts, comes in. Not only is McRoberts himself a great apologist for the Christian faith, but he is also a former student of Professor Montgomery. McRoberts also wrote a master's thesis on Montgomery's theological and apologetic thought. I know of no man alive today who is more equipped to author this monumental book, a work that will educate its readers on the legal-historical apologetic thought of the late John Warwick Montgomery."

— **Phil Fernandes, PhD**
Lead Pastor, Trinity Bible Fellowship,
Professor of Apologetics, Veritas International University,
Crosspoint Academy, and Northwest University (Kirkland, WA),
and President of the International Society of Christian Apologetics.

"Given Soloman's exhortation that writing many books is endless and excessive devotion to books wearies the body (Eccl 12:12) then why another book and why a book about John Warwick Montgomery who wrote over

70 books and 250 scholarly articles? The question is answered when Soloman contrasts the priority of God's Word and fearing God above all else as he writes, "fear God and keep His commandments because this applies to all persons" (Eccl 12:12). John Warwick Montgomery provides insight in how a man with such an incredible intellect and opportunity prioritized the historical accuracy and clarity of the Scripture and developed a model of theological inquiry that honored Jesus Christ.

When I was only 20 years-old and a brand-new believer in Christ with little Bible knowledge, I had to defend my personal faith during a very difficult and painful time of family rejection. As I started growing in my personal faith and learn more about The Faith, I began reading a few books by Dr. Montgomery. I am indebted to him and his contemporaries who defended the reliability, accuracy, and knowability of the Scripture and exemplified a sound, reasoned theological model that centralized the historical resurrection of Christ. McRobert's book, Faith Founded on Fact distills this truth about Dr. Montgomery.

Whether a person desires to read about refuting Bultmannian existentialism and the post-Bultmannian New Hermeneutic which is so popular today as advocated by post-modernists or skimming a reasoned rebuttal of Ludwig Wittgenstein's god-talk thesis or learning about the limitations of Kant's philosophy of history (or any other rationalistic philosophy of history, e.g., Hegel, Marx, Toynbee), this book will not be a disappointment.

But the crown jewel of the book is to grasp how Dr. Montgomery with his brilliant intellect, simply prioritizes the trustworthiness, preservation and knowability of the Old and New Testament from which he develops the Christian worldview to defend The Faith – and any believer (scholar or not, mature seasoned believer or new believer, academician or practitioner) can read this outstanding, accessible work by Dr. McRoberts that overviews the contributions of John Warwick Montgomery. I commend Dr. McRoberts for writing Faith Founded on Fact in such a readable manner and recommend this text to all who believe Faith can and should be defended in a reasonable manner."

— David A. Mappes, PhD
Professor of Biblical Studies at Liberty University,
Columbia International University (CIU), Calvary University (CU),
College of Biblical Studies (CBS), Chafer Theological Seminary and Veritas
International University (VIU) and Founder/Director of Nobility
and Knowability Truth Ministries (https://www.davidmappes.com/).

"I had already become fascinated with the work of Dr. John Montgomery, as Dr. McRoberts was, during my seminary years, which furthered my interest in the subject of apologetics. Dr. Montgomery and my careers seem to go side by side since we both taught and wrote on the topic of apologetics and worked in the area of law. I had the good fortune to have contact with him due to my subsequent teaching at Simon Greenleaf School of Law and Apologetics, which he began and developed, as well as Trinity Law School, which emerged from Simon Greenleaf. Moreover, during my concurrent teaching in Strasbourg, France, on the topic of international human rights, at the time that he conducted his popular course in apologetics one summer, I spent some time with him. He had a positive impact on my thinking. Without question, he is at the top of the list of apologists for the Christian faith, due to his books, teaching, and public debate. He was unflinching in his commitment to the evidential defense of Christianity and a commitment to Human Rights. Dr. Kerry McRoberts has performed an admirable task in introducing Dr. Montgomery and his ideas to many who might not know his work and importance in the defense of the Christian faith. I commend this book to all who desire to receive a careful and helpful introduction to the contribution of Dr. Montgomery's defense of the Christian faith and his advocacy of human rights. I applaud Dr. McRoberts for writing this book and encourage the reader to carefully read *Faith Founded on Fact*."

— **H. Wayne House, Th.D., J.D., Ph.D. (A.B.D)**
Distinguished Research Professor of Theology, Apologetics,
and Biblical Archaeology, Faith International University, Faith Seminary.

'FAITH FOUNDED ON FACT'

In Honor of the Legal-Historical Apologetics
of John Warwick Montgomery

KERRY D. McROBERTS

Foreword: Brian Nixon, D.PHIL.

LAMPION
House Publishing

LAMPION HOUSE PUBLISHING LLC
Navasota, Texas 77868

2025

Lampion House Publishing LLC
P.O. Box 1295
Navasota, TX 77868
Website: http://lampionhousepublishing.com/

Printed in the United States of America

ISBN: 979-8-9918278-3-6 (softcover)

First Edition, November 2025

David Mappes (Ph.D., Dallas Theological Seminary). Content Editor for Lampion House Publishing. See publications and various conference papers at https://www.davidmappes.com/

Cover and interior design/formatting by Vickie Swisher, Studio 20|20

CONTENTS

IN MEMORY OF
JOHN WARWICK MONTGOMERY

October 18, 1931 – September 25, 2024

John Warwick Montgomery was a lawyer – British barrister-at-law of the Middle Temple and Lincoln's Inn, England, member of the California, Virginia, Washington State, and District of Columbia Bars and the Bar of the Supreme Court of the United States. In addition to his legal career, Dr. Montgomery was a theologian, apologist – *par excellence,* philosopher, historian, ethicist and renown authority on International Law (Montgomery was an internationally recognized authority in several academic disciplines).

Professor Montgomery's teaching career included several distinguished schools to include the University of Chicago, Trinity Evangelical Divinity School, the International School of Law, Washington D.C. and the Simon Greenleaf School of Law, of which he was founder and dean. In his final stages of life, Professor Montgomery filled the post of Principal Lecturer in Law, Luton College of higher Education, London, England. And Dr. Montgomery continued until his death to direct the annual summer program at the International Seminar in Theology and Law, Strasbourg, France.

John Warwick Montgomery held 12 academic degrees, and he authored 70 books and 250 scholarly journal articles. Adam Francisco, Scholar in Residence at 1517, in his eulogy, wrote of how Dr. Montgomery "... traveled around the globe, leading reformation history tours, climbing Mount Ararat, and defending evangelists from persecution in places like Moldova and Turkey.

He more than dabbled in computer science and had interesting conversations with President Anwar Sadat, Israeli Prime Minister Menachem Begin, and the Hashemite King of Jordan. He even exchanged letters with C.S. Lewis."[1]

---

1   Adam Francisco, DPhil, Director of Academics and Scholar in Residence, https://www.1517. org/articles/john-warwick-montgomery-apologist-par-excellence. Downloaded: 02/26/2025.

FAITH FOUNDED ON FACT — BACKGROUND

My first encounter with John Warwick Montgomery was as an explorer. As a child I watched the documentary *In Search of Noah's Ark*. In the film — and later a book, *The Quest for Noah's Ark* — Dr. Montgomery led us on an exploration of Biblical proportions.

Dr. John Warwick Montgomery later became my professor at The Simon Greenleaf School of Law where I completed an MA in Apologetics. I completed a second MA in Systematic Theology at Regent College, Vancouver, Canada. Dr. J.I Packer was my thesis advisor at Regent; my thesis is entitled, "Faith Founded on Fact: The Apologetic Theology of John Warwick Montgomery."

Faith Founded on Fact, In Honor of The Legal-Historical Apologetics of John Warwick Montgomery is a rewrite/revision of my M.A. thesis. Dr. Montgomery's profound influence on my worldview, my writing and teaching has contributed much to my life and the lives of my students, churches, readers, and a large variety of antagonists to the Christian faith.

FOREWORD

BRIAN NIXON, D.PHIL.

Chief Academic Officer (CAO)
Veritas International University
&
Professor of Education
and Pastoral Studies

"Augustine," Brian, "Augus-tin!" Not "August-tean." So goes one of a handful of small interjections Dr. John Warwick Montgomery would toss my way every now and then.

Another I remember: "Brian, don't lean so heavily on Scripture, reason, and history as your theological guides, as good as they may be. For in the end, various groups will prioritize one over the other. Always stand on Scripture — first and foremost."

As small as these corrections may be, they are clear examples that John Warwick Montgomery valued truth, as supported by evidence from history, law, linguistics, science, and most importantly, the Bible.

Facts mattered to Montgomery, and they should matter to all Christians.

I had the honor of knowing and studying the work of Dr. Montgomery, a giant of evangelical thought. I consider him as one of the top intellectual influences on my life and of the 20th Century. Through his books, lectures, and keen intellectual insight, his impact will be felt for many years. After speaking at my graduation in Canterbury, England, I continued my connection with Dr. Montgomery through regular contact. So more than an intellectual mentor, he became a friend.

I'm not the only one he impacted.

In this masterful summary of Montgomery's thought, Kerry McRoberts has done the church a great service: He's given us a readable overview of Montgomery's intellectual vision, tackling Montgomery's view of history, theology, and apologetics.

Here's the thing. Like me, McRoberts knew and studied with Montgomery. But McRobert's had the double honor of Dr. J.I. Packer as his supervisor of this work. Imagine that: one of the greatest evangelical scholars giving insight into another great evangelical scholar. Amazing!

And when you add the Scotsman, Dr. James Houston, as the "Reader" of the work, you know you're dealing with marvelous information.

I know all of this because Dr. McRoberts was kind enough to mail me the original theses this work was based upon at Regent College in Vancouver, BC. And there before me are the signatures of both Packer and Houston.

To say the least, I encourage — and implore you — to read this work. Not only is it important on its own two feet, introducing you to the thought of Montgomery; but it highlights the work of a man whose shoes can hardly be filled, feet that trod evangelical truth, walking the bridge between C.S. Lewis and our contemporary age.

I know this. I tried to follow Montgomery as we browsed an "Antiquarian bookstore" — as he liked to call them — in Albuquerque, New Mexico. In his arms he had books on computer science, gastronomy, theology, history, and cars. Yep. He was a Renaissance man. And I've been playing catch-up ever since, following the path of a man who yearned with all his being to follow the Son of Man, Jesus our Lord.

SPECIAL DEDICATION

"A wife of noble character who can find?"
"She is clothed with strength and dignity;
She speaks with wisdom,
and faithful instruction is on her tongue." "
Many women do noble things, but you surpass them all."
"Honor her for all that her hands have done,
and let her works bring her praise at the city gate"
— Proverbs 31:10, 25a, 26, 28, 29, 31.

If the value of ministry — teaching, pastoral, and writing — was measured in terms of the value of precious gems, like Proverbs 31:10b, my calling would be worth far more than diamonds to me; but you, Vicki, in your strength, and dignity, would ever be the sparkle in those diamonds.

You speak with wisdom, and faithful instruction, but unlike any pastor's wife I have ever known of, you are very "unconventional" — You were, as a police officer, more at home in a police "bullpen" than a Women's Ministry gathering. You faithfully love the church, but you also loved Corvallis, Oregon — But how can a pastor's wife also be a cop without compromising one, or both vocations? Your first love is Jesus Christ, and in everything, you do life "in the name of the Lord Jesus" (Colossians 3:17).

"Many women do noble things, but..." in your unconventional ways, *"you surpass them all."* A Challenge Coin is awarded to a police officer or Crime Intel Analyst for meritorious achievement in a high-profile police operation. You were awarded a Challenge Coin, as the Crime Intel Analyst, for your meritorious service

involved with an abduction, homicide featured nationwide on ABC's 2020 News Magazine. You were awarded a second Challenge Coin for your integral role in bringing a serial murderer to justice in Portland, Oregon. And you received a third Challenge Coin for your role in "Operation Ice Breaker," a drug cartel investigation. (You were awarded two other Challenge Coins). And twice you were "Corvallis Police Employee of the Year (2002 & 2003).

Honor her for all that her hands have done, and let her works bring her praise at the city gate — over the span of several years, a progressive, university community witnessed "Christ in you, the hope of glory" (Colossians 1:27.) *"Her children arise, and call her blessed; her husband also, and he praises her"* — Vicki McRoberts, you are exceedingly "worth far more than rubies" (cf. Proverbs 31:10b).

INTRODUCTION

What is the relationship between the meaning of your life and a Christian philosophy of history?

In his signature work, *Faith Founded on Fact*, John Warwick Montgomery queries: "Are You Having A Fuddled Easter?" Montgomery concludes with an exhortation: "Let's stop the fuddlement. Let's go beyond A.H. Ackley's '"You ask me how I know he lives? He lives within my heart,' and proclaim to a lost society that Jesus lives in our hearts because he first of all rose in the very history in which we are embedded."[2] Pietists, like Ackley, "befuddle" Easter because they are apparently unaware of the historical significance of Christian faith.

This is to say, Christian historiography — i.e., the writing of history; the study of techniques involved with historical research — requires that both sacred or salvation-history e.g., the miraculous life of Jesus Christ) and ordinary or general history (e.g., from "(9-11, 2001, to the beginning of the life of any human being, cf. Jeremiah 29:11) are thoroughly wed together and can be written objectively. For example, Paul writes (1 Corinthians 15:3-5): "For what I received I passed on to you as of first importance: that Christ died for our sins according to the Scriptures, that he was buried, that he was raised on the third day according to the Scriptures, and that he appeared to Cephas, and then to the Twelve."

---

2   John Warwick Montgomery. *Faith Founded on Fact. Essays in Evidential Apologetics*. Nashville, TN: Thomas Nelson, Inc. 1978. 79.

The miraculous event of the Resurrection was "on the third day," an ordinary day in space, time, and history. The risen Lord *appeared*, the verb is first aorist passive indicative, which means, this was not a vision, it was an *actual appearance initiated* by Jesus Christ[3] "to Cephas (Peter) and then to the Twelve"!

The significance of this is colossal, "On one major point virtually all theologians of history — past and present — are in agreement: '... the meaning of general history is to be found in Jesus Christ.'"[4] Every ordinary historical event daily gravitates towards the ultimate ("Kairos") events in human history: Creation, the Incarnation, "Good Friday" — the Cross, and Easter Sunday (Gen.1:1; Jn. 1:1,14,18; Rom. 4:25). The relationship between the meaning of human life and Christian philosophy of history highlights Part 1 — "Knowable Reality."

"Knowable Reality" sets the table for Part 2 — "Theological Theory Formation." John Warick Montgomery demonstrates how theological models represent substantive-conceptual reality (i.e., "reality as it is"). The relationship between theological truth and knowable reality is tested in Part 3 — "Verifying JWM's Legal-Historical Methodology": Professor Montgomery argues that "One can confidently rely on [historical] fact to support faith. The appropriate method of disciplined empirical enquiry into the fact, or reality, of the person and life of Jesus Christ, according to Montgomery, is that which is codified by lawyers for the purpose of assessing evidence in a court of law.

Part 4 — At the conclusion of his magnum opus, *Tractatus Logico-Theologicus*, Montgomery responds to Ludwig Wittgenstein's analytical philosophical inspired *silence*, implying the meaninglessness of "god-talk," in the closing of his *Tractatus Logico-Philosophicus* — "What we cannot speak about we must pass over in

---

3   Archibald Thomas Robertson, *Word Pictures In The New Testament*. Grand Rapids, MI: Baker Book House, 1931.Vol. IV. The Epistles of Paul. Ch. XV. 187.

4   John Warwick Montgomery. *Where Is History Going?* 185.

silence" (7). Montgomery counters Wittgenstein, (perhaps proclaiming: "Au contraire!") — "Whereof one *can* speak, thereof one must *not* be silent" (7).

PART 1:

'KNOWABLE REALITY'

CHAPTER ONE

HOW CAN WE "SEE THE WORLD ARIGHT"?

"What we cannot speak about we must pass over in silence"
— Ludwig Wittgenstein.

Analytical philosopher, Ludwig Wittgenstein, was a rare genius. Wittgenstein "confessed" in his philosophical *magnum opus, Tractatus Logico-Philosophicus*, that, "My propositions serve as elucidations in the following way: anyone who understands me eventually recognizes them as nonsensical, when he has used them — as steps — to climb up beyond them. (He must, so to speak, throw away the ladder after he has climbed up it). He must transcend these propositions, and then he will see the world aright" — *"What we cannot speak about we must pass over in silence"* (*TLP* 6.54/7).[5]

Wittgenstein's "silence" is preceded by his supposition of God's "silence," in other words, the analytic philosophical consensus is that "god-talk" is meaningless. Wittgenstein's "silence"

---

[5]   Ludwig Wittgenstein. *Tractatus Logico-Philosophicus*. Translated by D.F. Pears and B.F. McGuinness. Routledge: London. 1974 (First paperback edition). 6.54. 7 Re: Closing thought (7). (Italics are mine).

determines the bounds of his reality: "*The limits of my language* mean the limits of my world" (*TLP* 5.6) — That is, whatever can be expressed in words demarcates the boundaries of *knowable* reality. However, despite his personal philosophical "gag order;" because of a supposed mute deity ("so to speak"), Wittgenstein acutely acknowledged: "The sense of the world must lie outside the world" (*TLP* 6.41). From the vantage point of his "ladder's" highest step, Wittgenstein contemplated his predicament in a formerly unpublished lecture, that later appeared in *Philosophical Review,* January 1965:

> And now I must say that if I contemplate what Ethics really would have to be if there were such a science, this result seems to me quite obvious. It seems to me obvious that nothing we could ever think or say should be *the* thing. That we cannot write a scientific book, the subject matter of which could be intrinsically sublime and above all other subject matters. I can only describe my feeling by the metaphor, that, if a man could write a book on Ethics which really was a book on Ethics, this book would, with an explosion, destroy all the other books in the world.[6]

Orthodox Christian faith earnestly contends, "that in Holy Scripture just such a book exists: A Book 'intrinsically sublime and above all other subject matters' because its Author is the transcendent Lord God, who is unconditioned by the human predicament that corrupts even our best attempts to find life's meaning, and who alone knows and is Absolute Truth."[7]

---

6   Ibid., *Philosophical Review.* "Lecture on Ethics" (Part Two). Vol. 74. Number 1. Edited by Sage School of Philosophy, Cornell University. Also: John Warwick Montgomery. *The Suicide of Christian Theology.* Minneapolis, MN: Bethany Fellowship INC. 1970. 366. And Ludwig Wittgenstein. "Lecture on Ethics." Delivered in November 1929 to the "Heretics Society." Cambridge University. Pp. 2-3 of 6 pages.

7   John Warwick Montgomery. *The Suicide of Christian Theology.* 366.

But is the Bible *really* God's revelation — His personal unveiling; and if the Bible is, "as Christians claim," would we then be able to transcend Wittgenstein's propositions and "see the world aright" in the Scriptures?

WHAT IS THE RELATIONSHIP BETWEEN DIVINE REVELATION & HISTORY?

"The Christian revelation satisfies the deepest general and particular longings of the human heart"
— John Warwick Montgomery, *Tractatus Logico-Theologicus*. 6.

Few theologians have done more to illumine the nature of the relationship between history and God's revelation than John Warwick Montgomery. Montgomery's reconstruction of a Christian historiography requires that both sacred or salvation-history (*heilsgeschichte*) and ordinary or general history (*historie*) are thoroughly wed and can be written objectively.

A reconstruction of Christian historiography — i.e., the writing of history; the study of techniques involved with historical research — leads to the rediscovery of cognitivity and truth in religious language, more specifically, the Christian faith. In his book, *The Shape of the Past*, John W. Montgomery points to a modern view, expounded by a French political journalist and commentator, Raymond Aron:

If I am a rationalist, I am a rationalist who ... recognizes the specific character of different spiritual universes.... Belief in the transcendent, even if I do not agree with it myself, seems to me to be a human activity of a particular type with a significance I can perceive. But when belief touches

5

on matters within the jurisdiction of empirical study and sociological analysis, I am convinced that it presents an entirely different aspect, and its falsity is easily demonstrated simply because it deals with values inaccessible to science.[8]

To many secular historians and philosophers of history, Christian historiography is laden with "values inaccessible to science." The secular historian concludes, *a priori*, that any attempt at a Christian philosophy of history must be considered meaningless because such efforts originate at the point of one's personal faith, a dimension removed from objective investigation and consequent verification. Therefore, in the minds of many modern philosophers and historians, theological assertions are meaningless because they are unsupportable in the real world of objective fact.

Montgomery acknowledges Wittgenstein for his penetrating assertion that "the sense of the world must lie outside the world"[9] — If we are, "Lacking the eternal perspective necessary to discover history's meaning, we must forever remain in darkness concerning it unless a shaft of light from outside the world illumines the shadows of history."[10] What is the relationship between revelation and history? Can historical inquiry yield objective knowledge (*fides historica*) of Christian revelatory events?

RECONSTRUCTING OBJECTIVE HISTORY

A Christian approach to historiography requires that both sacred or salvation-history and ordinary or general history can be written objectively.[11] For the sake of clarity, it would be helpful to state what Montgomery *does not* mean by "objective" history. Mont-

---

8   Aron, *L'histoire et ses interpretations*. 164-65. John Warwick Montgomery. *The Shape of the Past*. 138.

9   Ludwig Wittgenstein. *Tractatus Logico-Philosophicus*. 6.41. Ibid. 139.

10   John Warwick Montgomery. *Where Is History Going?* 140.

gomery does not mean (1) that historical knowledge is free from the value judgments of the historian[12] or (2) that the historian is merely a passive observer of the past, detached as it were, from his own *a priori* Weltanschauung.

What Montgomery *does* mean by objective history is that historical writing is open to criticism: "Thus for me, the question, 'How objective can history be?'" settles on the question, "To what extent is a systematic historical reconstruction exposed to criticism?"[13] Essential to Montgomery's view of historical objectivity is not freedom from value-judgments but rather the justification for such judgments, i.e., are "value-judgments" open to criticism and subject to reassessment in relation to the facts or events of history?[14]

The afore-question raises two critical issues concerning historical objectivity: (1) How does the historian go about the selection of his material? And (2) What is the relation between the facts of history and interpretation? Professor Montgomery appeals to J.A.

---

11   Paul D. Feinberg. "History: Public or Private? A Defense of John Warwick Montgomery's Philosophy of History." *Christian Scholar's Review*. I, 4 (Summer 1971). In John Warwick Montgomery. *The Shape of the Past*. 375.

12   Ibid. 13-17; 73. Montgomery argues that history, free from value-judgments, is impossible. It is for this very reason that Montgomery insists upon the need of history's openness to criticism (Ibid).

13   John W. Montgomery. *Where is History Going?* 194-95.

14   Montgomery's thought is supported by Wittgenstein, "If language is to be a means of communication there must be agreement not only in definition but also (queer as this may sound) in judgments." Ludwig Wittgenstein. *Philosophical Investigations*. 3rd ed., trans. by G.E.M. Anscombe. New York: Macmillan Co. 1968. Sect. 242, 88e.

      J.W.N. Watkins is cited by Montgomery for his rejection of the historical positivism of Baker and Walsh and his perceptive support of the traditional historical understanding of historical reconstruction:

      My own belief is that, while it is no doubt desirable that the historian should be as aware as possible of the sources of potential bias within himself, what really matters, in connection with the problem of historical objectivity, is not so much the historian's mentality as the logical structure of what he writes. The regulative moral and metaphysical convictions, the passion and controversy, which Walsh regards as the causes and symbols of subjectivity in history, have their counterparts in the natural sciences, which Walsh regards as paradigms of objectivity. The objective character of a scientific theory is not a function of its author's temperament and mentality, but of its *criticizability*. Thus, for me, the question "How objective can history be?" The question, "To what extent is a systematic historical reconstruction exposed to criticism?" must immediately follow. "Philosophy of History: Publication in English." In, *La Philosophie au milieu du vingtieme siècle*. Ed. Raymond Klibansky. 4 Vols., 2d ed.; Firenze, 1961-62, II, 174. In, John Warwick Montgomery. *Where Is History Going?* 171.

Pasmore's astute insight into the historian's method of selecting his material:

> The determining factor, I have suggested, must be the na-
> ture of the problem from which he sets out, just as it is
> in the case of the physical scientist. There is, however, an
> important difference in character of his problems; histori-
> cal problems are more like a certain type of problem in ap-
> plied science than they are like problems in pure science.
> This consequence of the fact that the historian is interest-
> ed in what happens in a particular situation on a particu-
> lar occasion; just as an engineer may have to ask himself:
> "Why did 'that' aeroplane collapse?" so the historian asks:
> "Why did 'that' monarchy collapse?" Furthermore, again
> like the engineer, he may, usually does, solve his problem
> by constructing a model.[15]

The historical model constructed by the historian is based on the accepted canons of historiography — canons that are a part of the historical inquiry, without regard to the historian's own personal inclinations or convictions. But what explanation can be offered by historians for the diversity of accounts involving the same historical event? Again, Montgomery appeals to Passmore who alludes to some of the aforementioned historiographical can-ons as part of his explanation:

> What ought to surprise and gratify us is the extent to
> which the spirit of objectivity has won its triumphs. Ro-
> man Catholic and Protestant accounts of the Reforma-
> tion, considered as a story about social institutions, come
> more and more into conformity. If the test for objectivity
> is that there are regular ways of settling issues, by the use of

---

15   J.A. Passmore. *Philosophical Analysis and History*. Ed. William H. Dray. New York: Harper & Row. 1966. 75-94. John Warwick Montgomery. Ibid., 172.

which men of whatever party can be brought to see what actually happened, then I do not see how one can doubt the objectivity of history. But if we are satisfied with nothing less than the production of histories which all men the least rational will accept as final, then that would be a greater victory for the scientific spirit than we have any reason to expect. Such unanimity, however, is not to be found in any branch of human inquiry. Once again, if we press the criterion of objectivity too hard, it applies to no form of inquiry; slacken it slightly and history edges its way in with the rest.[16]

Montgomery does not hesitate to acknowledge the possibility of multiple interpretations of any one historical event.[17] This is not an issue of grave concern where objectivity is involved.

On the contrary, objectivity is preserved by the fact that the event itself provides us with adequate criteria to choose the *correct* interpretation from among the variety of possible interpretations. Thus, Montgomery's case for historical objectivity is based on the historian's coherent reconstruction of the facts of a given historical event:

Indubitably, in our contingent world there are an infinite number of *possible* interpretations and value judgements for any single historical fact.... But, just as obviously, not all explanations are equally plausible, and diverse interpretations and value judgements can and must be examined against the facts themselves. In the process, less satisfactory judgments will go by the board, and one will arrive at an interpretation as to meaning and significance that best fits the facts under analysis....[18]

---

16   Ibid.
17   Ibid. 163.
18   Ibid. 163-64.

How are plausible or correct historical interpretations concluded? Or to be more precise, what is the relation between the facts of history and their interpretation?

HISTORY'S OBJECTIVITY & THE PUBLIC NATURE OF FACTS

Montgomery's "conviction that historical facts do carry their interpretations, i.e., that facts in themselves provide adequate criteria for choosing among variant interpretations of them, is essential both to the Christian and to general historiography."[19] Meanings involved with historical facts are public (objective and public are used here synonymously), and therefore the facts of a particular historical event provide adequate criteria for their specific application. It must be stressed that the conviction that historical facts and interpretations are inseparable is in keeping with contemporary historiography.[20]

Wittgenstein stresses, "One cannot guess how a word functions. One has to look at its use and learn from that."[21] George Pitcher's comments extend clarification to Wittgenstein's thought:

---

19   Ibid. 164.

20   The inseparability of facts and their meanings is also cogently argued for by Wolfhart Pannenberg of the University of Munich in his, *Revelation as History*. New York: Macmillan. 168. And *Faith and Reality*. Philadelphia, Westminster. 1977. The alternative to this view is the positivist's search for bare brute facts apart from any interpretation which ends in a relativistic meaninglessness. Thus, theologian James Robinson argues:

Such a splitting up of historical consciousness into a detection of facts and an evaluation of them (or into history as known and history as experienced) is intolerable to Christian faith, not only because the message of the resurrection of Jesus and of God's revelation in him necessarily becomes merely subjective interpretation, but also because it is the reflection of an outmoded and questionable historical method. It is based on the futile aim of the positivist historians to ascertain bare facts without meaning in history.

"The Revelation of God in Jesus." *Theology as History*. Ed. James Robinson and John B. Cobb, Jr. New York: Harper & Row, 1967. 126-27.

21   Ludwig Wittgenstein. *Philosophical Investigations*. Sec. 340. Paul D. Feinberg. *History: Public Or Private? A Defense of John Warwick Montgomery's Philosophy of History*. In John Warwick Montgomery. *The Shape of the Past*. 377.

What determines whether the word's "meaning" and "understanding" can appropriately be applied to a person **P** in any given situation is the nature of the situation and its wider context — for example, what sort of person **P** is, how much **P** knows about the matter at hand, what it is he is alleged to mean or understand, what led up to the situation, and especially how **P** does, or would under suitable conditions, act after the situation. What goes on in **P**'s mind, if anything, is rarely, if ever, the circumstance which warrants the correct application of the terms "meaning" and "understanding."[22]

Following from the Wittgensteinian understanding of public meanings, the idea of historical fact is used synonymously with historical event by Montgomery.[23] Therefore, as opposed to private or personal meanings, the criteria for an historical event must be satisfied by the event itself and must consist of both verbal and non-verbal behavior.[24] This is explicitly what Montgomery means by the self-interpreting nature of historical facts or events. If the event provides the historian with adequate criteria for choosing among the variety of possible interpretations, then there must be an *empirical necessity* that unites an event or fact with its correct interpretation. In support of Montgomery's insistence that facts must not be separated from their meanings, George Ladd provides a lucid illustration drawn from two statements:[25]

(a) Jesus died.

(b) Jesus died for the sins of the world.

---

22 George Pitcher. *The Philosophy of Wittgenstein.* Englewood Cliffs: Prentice Hall. 1964. 257. John Warwick Montgomery. Ibid.

23 Ludwig Wittgenstein. *Philosophical Investigations.* Sections 199-300. Feinberg. *History: Public Or Private?*

24 Ibid. 377.

25 George Ladd. *I Believe in the Resurrection of Jesus.* Grand Rapids: Eerdmans. 1975. 18ff.

Christians believe both (a) and (b) statements to be true. Further, both (a) and (b) are objective in the sense that they happened in the real world. However, though (a) and (b) are objective in the one sense, only (a) was publicly observable by an individual present at Golgatha to see the death of Jesus of Nazareth. That is, anyone present could have seen Jesus die on that Friday afternoon but no one present could actually have *seen* Christ's atonement for the sins of the world. In that sense, (b) is not a straightforward historical claim as (a) is.

Herein lies the crux of the matter involving the public nature, i.e., the self-interpreting character of historical facts: (b) "Jesus died for the sins of the world," is not so much a historical claim, as (a) "Jesus died," as it is an interpretation of what took place outside the walls of Jerusalem on mount Calvary. The atonement, the interpretation of Jesus' death is offered as a part of the public record (e.g., the Gospels) handed down to man as Special Revelation. The Bible, in keeping with the criterion of a classical historiography, uniquely provides the Christian with an inspired interpretation of the historical events of Scripture.[26]

The separation of fact from meaning requires the interpretation or meaning of the Gospel (or any historical event) to be

---

26   In his, "Defending the Gospel Through the Centuries," (Institute for Law & Gospel, Newport Beach, CA.; Cassette Album), Montgomery provides several examples. For example, Luke 1:26-38 records the appearance of the angel Gabriel to Mary to announce the virgin birth of Jesus Christ. Not only is the announcement made, the angel interprets the event in detail. The event is significant because the child Jesus "will be great and will be called the Son of the Most High. The Lord God will give him the throne of his father David, and he will reign over the house of Jacob forever; his kingdom will never end." And Mary inquirers of the angel, "How will this be, ... since I am a virgin?" The angel responds, "The Holy Spirit will come upon you and the power of the Most High will overshadow you" (vv. 32-35). In speaking of the crucifixion of Jesus Christ, the Apostle John (Jn. 19:37) interprets the significance of the event in detail and informs us, as a part of his interpretation of the event, "These things happened so that the scripture would be fulfilled" (v. 36). Montgomery's point is that the Scripture does not leave room for positivistic interpretations of the historical events that provide the setting for the acts of the living God.

private or "hidden."[27] A positivistic historiography reduces Christianity to a particular religious way of perceiving reality.[28]

Kant's philosophy of history (or any other rationalistic philosophy of history, e.g., Hegel, Marx, Toynbee) holds four outstanding flaws, according to Montgomery: (1) it is incapable of establishing a necessitarian character;[29] (2) it is unable to justify value judgments, in absolute terms, concerning what is significant and valuable with respect to a philosophy of history; (3) the optimistic view of human nature, held particularly by Kant, is an unjustified and unprovable concept and; (4) ethical presuppositions (e.g., Kant's view that the end justifies the means) are strictly gratuitous.[30]

Classical historiography asserts that the meaning of a historical event has its ground in history.[31] Hence, although positivist historians insist on the separation of facts and their interpretation, secular and Christian philosophers of history are increasingly seeing the critical need to conjoin fact and meaning in historical investigation. The reason for this is that such a view appears "forced

---

27 In his eighth proposition, Kant asserted that "the history of the human race, viewed as a whole, may be regarded as the realization of a hidden plan of nature to bring about a political constitution, internally, and, for this purpose, also externally perfect, as the only state in which all the capacities implanted by her in mankind can be fully developed." Immanuel Kant. "Idea of a Universal History from a Cosmopolitan Point of View." Trans. W. Hastie. Reprinted in Patrick Gardiner, ed. *Theories of History.* Glencoe, Ill.: Free Press, 1959. 30. John Warwick Montgomery. *Where Is Going?* 17.

28 Positivism presupposes that all genuine knowledge derived by reason and logic from sensory experience, are based on "positive" data of experience; that is, theories that are built on positivism see the world 'as it is' (i.e., a direct correspondence between one's perception and the world is a fundamental assumption of positivism). Therefore, according to logical positivism, metaphysical propositions express truth that is not only wrong and/or false but meaningless. The French scholar, Auguste Comte, originated the term 'positivism' in the 1820s.

29 That is, the system does not grow out of history itself but is rather a philosophical imposition, i.e., an artificial imposition, on history itself. Elsewhere Montgomery has argued: "But 'confidence in history' is laudable if it means that, over against existential and solipsistic skepticism, one confidently endeavors to find the meaning of historical events by objective study of the events themselves. Only in this way can one avoid imposing a philosophy, as a Procrustean bed, on the past. If the Christian philosophy of history is truly valid, it must arise from within history itself. And it does: for it derives from the historical Christ." Ibid. 166.

30 Ibid. 30.

31 Ibid. 166.

upon the subject by the nature of the material with which he is dealing."[32]

Indeed, as to its nature, the Bible is more than a mere history book. It is rather the history of revelation and the nature of Scripture forces one to regard Christian historiography as more properly a theology of history.[33]

Regarding a Christian philosophy of history, Montgomery acknowledges the normative implications of the Bible:

> It seems to me that a Christian philosophy of history has to begin with the assumption that there are objective events which do indeed carry their interpretation with them. This is true not only of the events of biblical history but of the events of history in general. If then we ask, "why do we need the Bible to help us to interpret history?" the answer is that such a welter of historical data exist that we do not know how to relate all the facts to each other. Our lifetime is too short and our perspective is too limited. By way of Scripture, we are able to enter the Christological heart of the historical process and thereby understand the operation of other events. We can use the biblical narratives — particularly the narratives concerning our Lord — as a criterion of significance and also a means of comprehending human nature and ethical values, so that we can see meaning in the totality of human life as displayed in history.[34]

---

32 Maurice Mandelbaum. *The Problem of Historical Knowledge*. New York: Harper & Row, 1967. 97.
    It should be noted that the context of Mandelbaum's comments involves his discussion of facts and their interpretation being considered in neither a subjective nor an objective manner. Whereas the subjective approach maintains that the interpretation of an event proceeds from the subject itself, the objective approach concludes that facts carry their own interpretation because of the nature of the material the historian is dealing with. This quote is intentionally used by me, the author, to reinforce Montgomery's position on the objectivity of history and the necessity of facts carrying their own interpretation.

33 John Calvin. *Institutes*. I, xvi, 3.

34 John Warwick Montgomery. *Where is History Going?* 203.

Special Revelation lays the foundation for Christian episte-mology. By means of Special Revelation, "we see 'historical Jesus' and 'kerygmatic Christ' thoroughly united, providing an objective ground — the only ground — for an interpretation of total history that is not subject to the limitations of man's sinful situation."[35]

HISTORICAL STATEMENTS ARE SYNTHETIC

Historical truth is synthetic, rather than analytic, i.e., history yields probable evidence of truth rather than rational proof as required by mathematics or formal logic. However, it is not the intention of classical Christian historiography to elevate religious truth above the supposed "incertitudes" of history (Tillich) as a means of countering the mere probability ridden nature of histo-ry. On the contrary, according to Montgomery, classical Christian historiography concludes that, "The empirical, historical evidenc-es in behalf of Christian revelation are not absolute (no synthetic proof can be)."[36] However, this is inconsequential for: "Probabil-ity argumentation is employed constantly by historians in their

---

35 Ibid. 197.

36 Ibid. 137-38. Ian Ramsey, through reference to Butler and Newman, is supportive of Montgom-ery's position concerning history and the nature of Christian truth:

Butler reminded us that a total devotion to duty — shown, for example by leaping into a river to save a drowning child — could and 'reasonably,' be associated with many empirical uncertainties and probabilities: we might be mistaken about the strength of the current, about our swimming ability, or whether in fact that floating heap was a child, and so on. But acknowledging these uncertainties Butler claimed that we should nevertheless think a man in a literal sense distracted — not himself — who failed to respond to the moral challenge displayed by such a situation of great consequence. For Butler this moral response reared on probabilities, this total devotion, and (in Newman's phrase) this "real assent" is reasonable, as being that which any "reasonable" man, anyone deserving to be called a person, would in similar circumstances display. "Probabili-ty" in this special sense is (said Butler) the "guide of life." So, our Christian convictions based on historical uncertainties are in principle reasonable as being one with the rest of life.

Ian Ramsey. *Christian Discourse: Some Logical Explorations*. London: Oxford University Press. 1965. 23-4.

work and must be relied upon if historical research is to have any meaning at all."[37]

Only synthetic judgments, based on empirical investigation in the form of historical research, can provide substantive knowledge of reality. Formal statements of absolute certainty (apodictic statements), offer no knowledge of the world at all. Consequently, recognition of the synthetic nature of historical affirmations is prerequisite to the verification question where Christian truth-claims are concerned.

A CHRISTIAN PHILOSOPHY OF HISTORY

A Christian philosophy of history always speaks of *heilsgeschichte* (salvation-history) within the context of ordinary history (*historie*).[38] The Epistle to the Hebrews (1:1-3) is a divinely inspired example of the relationship of *heilsgeschichte* and *historie*:

> *"In the past God spoke to our ancestors through the prophets at many times and in various ways, but in these last days he has spoken to us by his Son, whom he appointed heir of all things, and through whom also he made the universe. The Son is the radiance of God's glory and the exact representation of his being, sustaining all things by his powerful word. After he had provided purification for sins, he sat down at the right hand of the Majesty in heaven."*

Montgomery observes from the Hebrews letter that, "On the one hand, God works in general (ordinary) human history, for He

---

37 John Warwick Montgomery. *The Shape of the Past.* 139. See also, Montgomery, *Human Rights & Human Dignity*, 153-54 for a developed argument on this point.

38 Montgomery observes that "In this worldview, objective Time becomes the *total simul* — the eternal present — of God's love, and the Christ event becomes meaningful for men of past ages who looked forward to this salvation as well as for men of our present era who look back to it." *The Shape of the Past.* 29.

'upholds all things by the word of his power.' On the other, He has become part of man's story in a special way through prophetic revelation and the atoning sacrifice of Himself in the person of Jesus of Nazareth. Thus, Christian theology of history must always speak both of total history and of *Heilsgeschichte.*"[39]

Where is history going? What is the Christian answer to the destiny of mankind? Professor Montgomery explains the Christian conception of history in terms of the holy Trinity:

> The God of the Christian faith presents Himself as Father, Son, and Holy Spirit as Creator, Redeemer, and Sanctifier of man's historical life. The Christian understanding of history can be visualized as a line which begins with creation, centers on the redemptive act of God in Jesus Christ, and finds its termination in a sanctifying final judgment....[40]

God is both Creator and Preserver of the universe and Sovereign Lord over the stream of historical events that He has destined to fulfill His divine will on behalf of humanity. He is "not such as is imagined by sophists, vain, idle, and almost asleep, but vigilant, efficacious, operative, and engaged in continual action."[41]

For a Christian philosophy of history to be valid, it must itself arise from within the historical process. And this is the case, the meaning of history is centered in the person and work of Jesus Christ, God incarnate: "On one major point virtually all theologians of history — past and present — are in agreement: *the meaning of history is to be found in Jesus Christ.*"[42]

Thus, the "... Christian philosopher or historian will therefore do the cause of Christ no good by deemphasizing historical objec-

---

39   Montgomery. *Where is History Going?* 101.

40   Ibid. 32.

41   John Calvin. *Institutes.* I, xvi, 3.

42   Montgomery. *Where Is History Going?* 185.

tivity. If one is incapable of discovering the meaning of historical events from the events, then one is incapable of finding the divine Christ in history, and history will most certainly reduce to 'a tale told by an idiot, signifying nothing.'"[43]

Rather than taking a passive stance concerning the historical investigation of Christian truth-claims, Montgomery asserts the crucial need to appropriate the resurrected Christ of Christianity personally by faith:

> ... I say only that the historical probabilities are comparable to those of other events of classical times. Therefore, there is an excellent objective ground to which to tie the religion that Jesus sets forth. Final validation of this can only come experientially. But it is desperately important not to put ourselves in such a position that the event-nature of the resurrection depends wholly upon "the faith." It's the other way around. The faith has its starting point in the event, the objective event, and only by the appropriation of this objective event do we discover the final validity of it. The appropriation is the subjective element, and this must not enter into the investigation of the event. If it does, the Christian faith is reduced to irrelevant circularity.[44]

Personal assurance concerning the Resurrection of Christ does not come from a faith decision, which results in an "irrelevant circularity," but rather the foundation for faith is outside of faith in the historical event of the Resurrection. When the historian considers everything relevant to the context of the historical event of Christ's resurrection, that fact or event provides sufficient grounds for determining the meaning of the empty tomb. And therefore, since "Christianity ... declares that the truth of its absolute claims rests squarely on certain historical facts, open to

---

43   Ibid. 166.
44   Ibid. 238.

ordinary investigation ..."[45] — "One can confidently rely on fact to support faith. The privilege and responsibility exist to employ facts to lead today's seeking unbeliever to the faith once delivered to the saints."[46]

THE 'INSUPERABLE' PROBLEM WITH *A PRIORI* APPROACHES

A priori approaches to historical investigation, such as those of Christian presuppositionalists, insist that facts are not self-interpreting; consequently, they are inaccessible to the unregenerate. Cornelius Van Til, often referred to as the "Father of presuppositionalism," sets forth the presuppositionalist case as follows:

> All is yellow to the jaundiced eye. As he speaks of the facts the sinner reports them to himself and others as yellow every one. There are no exceptions to this. And it is the facts as reported to himself, that is as distorted by his own subjective condition, which he assumes to be the facts as they really are.[47]

Van Til continues his contention concerning the sinner's defective vision and subsequent inability to perceive intelligible facts that point to God:

> What then more particularly do I mean by saying that epistemologically the believer and the non-believer have nothing in common? I mean that every sinner looks through colored glasses. And these colored classes are cemented to this face. He assumes that self-consciousness is intelligible

---

45   John Warwick Montgomery. *Human Rights & Human Dignity.* 157.

46   Montgomery. *Faith Founded On Fact.* xxv.

47   Cornelius Van Til. "Introduction" in: *The Inspiration and Authority of the Bible.* By B.B. Warfield. Philadelphia: Presbyterian and Reformed Publishing Co. 1948. 20. John Warwick Montgomery. *Faith Founded On Fact.* 108.

without God-consciousness. He assumes that conscious-ness of facts is intelligible without consciousness of God.[48]

As long as the jaundiced condition of the sinner's eyes persists, because of his unregenerate condition, he is unable to properly interpret any fact within the purview of a divinely ordered history:

> Shall we in the interest of a point of contact admit that man can interpret anything correctly if he virtually leaves God out of the picture? Shall we who wish to prove that nothing can be explained without God, first admit that some things at least can be explained without him? On the contrary we shall show that all explanations without God are futile.[49]

However, if "there are no exceptions" and therefore, all facts are tainted with the same yellowish hue, then how is sinful man, a condition that affects Christian and non-Christian alike, able to distinguish reality from fantasy? Professor Montgomery draws the inescapable conclusion that, "if everyone without exception has colored glasses cemented to his face, no one can criticize another person's spectacles, or indeed the 'spectacle' of another worldview."[50]

Professor Montgomery's conclusions point to one presuppositionalist axiological ship passing the other *a priori* vessel of other competing world views in the night without the slightest degree of meaningful communication:

> But how do we choose among *a priori* positions? Each religion has its own *a prioris*, and many of the most fundamental tenets contradict those of other faiths. Without an

---

48   Cornelius Van Til. *A Christian Theory of Knowledge*. Philadelphia: Presbyterian and Reformed Publishing Co., 1969. 295. J.W. Montgomery. *Faith Founded On Fact*. 108.

49   Ibid. 294.

50   John Warwick Montgomery. *Faith Founded On Fact*. 111.

objective criterion, one is at a loss to make a meaningful choice among *a prioris*.[51]

A priori approaches to historiography reduce to meaningless tautological axioms (e.g., if **A** then **A**) involving no real matters of fact. They are therefore, as pointed out by Montgomery, quite incapable of reflecting any substantive reality at all in the world of fact:

> The moment we enter the realm of fact, we must depend on probability, this may be unfortunate, but it is unavoidable, and since it does not keep us from making decisions in non-religious matters, it should not immobilize us when religious commitment is involved.[52]

In fact, empirical methodology, as applied to historical investigation, leads to the climatic Christian assertion that the Son of the living God "rises from the dead — bodily — to manifest His *historisch* resurrection even to those such as Thomas who disbelieved." Moreover, "... when Adam heard the Lord's voice calling to him after the Fall, he was still able to interpret properly both the origin of the voice and its meaning; the Fall did not render Adam incapable of comprehending a word from God."[53]

Reflecting on the question-begging nature of *a priorism*, Montgomery queries: "... why should the non-Christian begin where the Christian begins?"[54] Montgomery's point is that *a priori* approaches to historical investigation reduce the Christian faith to "irrelevant circularity" — this is considered demonstrative of error in virtually all systems of thought except presuppositionalism

---

51   Montgomery. *The Shape of the Past*. 143.

52   Ibid. 143-144.

53   John Warwick Montgomery. *Faith Founded on Fact*. 122-23.

54   Montgomery. *Myth, Allegory and Gospel*. 17.

which considers it a sign of intellectual virtue.[55] But contrary to presuppositionalism's meaningless circularity, "In actual fact, it is not the defense of the gospel that makes God's truth irrelevant, but the refusal to defend it in the objective terms of the New Testament proclamation."[56]

It is noteworthy that Kant demonstrated that all arguments and systems necessarily begin with presuppositions. However, though this is the case, it does not follow that all presuppositions are equally desirable. Professor Montgomery argues that one should begin "with presuppositions of *method* (which yield truth) rather than with presuppositions of substantive *content*, (which assume a body of truth already").[57]

CONCLUSION

Concerning a Christian philosophy of history, Montgomery stresses:

Only the Christian faith... offers the historian (1) a reliable, absolute conception of human nature, (2) a criterion of historical importance (the Cross), (3) a knowledge of the origin and goal of history, and (4) a means of regeneration for the historian himself. Thus, evangelicals have a holy responsibility to lead present-day historiography out of its naturalistic blind alley; and if they neglect this task

---

55   See, for example, Cornelius Van Til's two works: *The Defense of the Faith*. Philadelphia: Presbyterian and Reformed. 1955. 118. And *A Survey of Christian Epistemology*. Den Dulk Foundation. 1969. 12. Van Til unashamedly concedes:

To admit one's own presuppositions and to point out the presuppositions of others is therefore to maintain that all reasoning is, in the nature of the case, *circular reasoning*. The starting point, the method, and the conclusions are always involved in one another. *A Christian Theory of Knowledge*. 25-26.

Quoted by R.C. Sproul. "The Case for Inerrancy: A Methodological Analysis." *God's Inerrant Word: An International Symposium on The Trustworthiness of Scripture*. Ed. John Warwick Montgomery. 246.

56   John Warwick Montgomery. *Faith Founded on Fact*. 32.

57   John W. Montgomery. *The Shape of the Past*. 141.

they are like the unheeding priest and Levite who "passed by on the other side" when radical need cried out to them on the way from Jerusalem to Jericho.[58]

The theological methodology of John Warwick Montgomery engages an empirical historiography as essential to Christian epistemology. Proper theological theory formation, according to Montgomery [and classical Lutheranism], "ought to be approached by way of the Incarnation and the Cross."[59]

REFORMED CLAIMS TO THE LIMITS OF THE EMPIRICAL METHOD

Does the empirical method, as applied to historical investigation, adequately yield theological truth concerning the historic Christian faith? Are historical facts necessarily self-interpreting if historical objectivity is going to be preserved? Or must historical objectivity be demonstrated *a posteriori* through the establishing of an independent theistic structure?

Professor Montgomery states that the methodology he employs for the purpose of verifying theological assertions is "an empirical argument based upon the application of historical method to an allegedly objective event." Montgomery continues, "Thus it provides no more than probable evidence for the truth of the

---

58   Montgomery. *Where Is History Going?* 13.
     Concerning secular historiography, Montgomery observes:
     ... secular historiography in our day has reached a philosophical impasse in at least four respects: (1) it is unable to arrive at a satisfactory and defensible conception of human nature; (2) it is unable, for want of an absolute axiology, to determine levels of significance among historical events; (3) it is unable to set out patterns of total history, since neither the origin nor the goal of history is known; and (4) it is unable, having no doctrine of regeneration, to tell the historian how to put into practice Croce and Collingwood's paramount dictum that the historian must re-experience the past, for re-experiencing requires a radical change in the egocentric personality of the historian, who tends to read his own personality back into the past instead of "losing himself" in order to "find" the people of past ages. Ibid.

59   Ibid. 160.

Christian worldview."[60] And therefore, "causation like the historical or scientific explanations that incorporate causal thinking, is no more than an empirical, synthetic construct which is employed *ad hoc* to deal with historical facts — Causal explanations are grounded in, and tested against, the facts for which they endeavor to account."[61]

Can an empirical method of historical investigation establish a logical necessity between alleged causes and their effects?[62] Philosophical realignments since the eighteenth century have added to science the grand assumption of the invariable correlation of cause-and-effect occurrences in the space-time world. But what about the extension of empirical inference and the assumption of causality to metaphysical realities? David Hume (1711-1776), the so-called, "last of the great triumvirate of British empiricists," speaks to the extension of empirical inference and the assumption of causality from within the inherent confines of Enlightenment dualism:

> The contention of David Hume was, of course, that one could not necessarily make a cause-and-effect. Hume was led to the conclusion that by means of empiricism, nothing normative can be known. Hume contended that if only that knowledge is valid which is acquired through sense experience (i.e., the empiricism of John Locke that characterized the Enlightenment, that is, the "Age of Reason" in Great Britain) then there is no valid knowledge of such fundamental matters as the notion of cause and

---

60   John Warwick Montgomery. *The Shape of the Past.* 139.

61   Montgomery. *Where Is History Going?* 71.
      Professor Montgomery adds: "Where normal causal explanations are wanting (e.g., in regard to the nature of light in physics or the nature of Christ's resurrection in history), no one properly rejects the objectivity of the phenomena. Light is still there, and so is the resurrection! Ibid.

62   In his *Essay Concerning Human Understanding*, John Locke, "the father of British empiricism," argued that the "passive mind" is central to the process of knowing. At birth, the mind is *tabula rasa*, i.e., a blank slate devoid of any innate ideas. The mind then formulates the impressions it receives from the external world through the senses into ideas.

effect or the idea of substance. Knowledge can never rise to the universal and the necessary if its starting point is the mere sense perceptions impressed on the mind by the external world; for flux only flux results. This epistemic starting point restricts one to merely describing a series of disjointed impressions, nothing more. Hume's skepticism then effectively reduced the possibility of knowing anything down to nothing.[63]

Hume's skepticism reduces knowledge to mere sense impressions upon the mind from the external world and consequently, knowledge can never rise to the universal and necessary.

Edward J. Carnell echoes Hume in his contention that, "One can never ascend to a demonstration of the immutable from evidence which the senses report, since they witness only to a succession of impressions."[64] Augustine's thoughts are (as are Max Black's) supportive of Carnell: "For whatever exists in some thing cannot endure unless that endures in which it exists. But we have just granted that truth endures even when true things pass away. Therefore, truth does not have its existence in mortal things."[65] If sense experience is foundational to knowledge, then all one can do, following from empiricism, is merely describe a series of disjointed impressions. Carnell bluntly concludes: "To take immutability from the mutable would out-Houdini Houdini."[66]

Montgomery counters the charges against empirical method:

---

63   Fredrick Copleston, S.J. *A History of Philosophy*. Volume V. "Hobbes to Hume." New Jersey: Paulist Press. 1959. 258-317. The revisions of this view by John Stuart Mill has opened the door for a cognition of the cause and effect relationship in the human mind.

64   Edward J. Carnell. *An Introduction to Christian Apologetics*. Grand Rapids: Wm. B. Eerdmans. 1956. 129. In support of Carnell, Max Black, Montgomery's philosophy mentor at Cornell, insists that the concept of cause is "a peculiar, unsystematic, and erratic notion," so that "any attempt to state a 'universal law of causation' must prove futile." Max Black. *Models and Metaphors*. 69. In John Warwick Montgomery. *Faith Founded On Fact*. 46-47.

65   *Soliloquia*. I.15.

66   Edward J. Carnell. *An Introduction To Christian Apologetics*. 129.

Historical investigation very definitely can take place on the empirical level without the positivistic presupposition that the nexus of natural causes cannot be broken. It seems to me that the question here is whether historical method, apart from that rationalistic presupposition, will or will not yield revelatory data concerning Jesus Christ. And if one says that it won't, then one strips away the meaning of the word "objectivity."[67]

Montgomery continues his explanation:

One meets in the primary documents a man who convinces both His friends and His enemies that He regards Himself as no less than God Incarnate, come to earth to die for the sins of the world. He places His stamp of divine approval on the Old Testament, as witnessing to Him, and promises His Holy Spirit to the apostles in order that the Spirit may bring to their remembrance all things that He had said to them (John 14:26). He rises from the dead — bodily — to manifest His *historisch* resurrection even to those such as Thoms who disbelieved. Here we see "historical Jesus" and "kerygmatic Christ" thoroughly united, providing objective ground — the only objective ground — for an interpretation of total history that is not subject to the limitations of man's sinful situation.[68]

The empirical method of Montgomery is *Christo-centric* and therefore, his method commences with historical investigation into the life, death and resurrection of a divine Person — One can confidently infer eternal realities from One of whom it can be said is "veiled in flesh the Godhead see" (cf. Jn. 1:1, 14; 14:9;

---

67   John Warwick Montgomery. *Where Is History Going?* 228.
68   Ibid. 196-197.

20:24-29, and Col. 2: 9). Is, therefore, an independent theistic structure necessary?

In his *Human Rights & Human Dignity*, Professor Montgomery confronts five preeminent theologians: "Finally, the objection may be offered: even granting Jesus' resurrection, is fact alone enough to establish His deity and the truth of His claims? Theological presuppositionists Carl F.H. Henry and Ronald H. Nash tell us that there are no self-interpreting facts, and Calvinists John Gerstner and R.C. Sproul, as well as Evangelical neo-Thomist Norman L. Geisler, insist that an independent theistic structure must be established to make any theological sense out of Jesus' resurrection. I profoundly disagree."[69]

The positing of an "independent theistic structure," that is, reasoning from knowledge of the Creator and thus reasoning from the "known" is *necessary*, in the thinking of Gerstner, Sproul and Geisler, for the purpose of imputing such meaning to the particulars in the earth as will include the entry of God Himself onto the historical plane. Norman Geisler explains this point of view and further, he [Geisler] remarks on another supposed problem in Montgomery's thought:

> First, facts and events have ultimate meaning only within and by virtue of the context of the worldview in which they are conceived. Hence, it is a vicious circle to argue that a given fact (say, the resuscitation of Christ's body) is

---

69   John Warwick Montgomery. *Human Rights & Human Dignity*. 156.

The problems with *a priori* arguments have been discussed in this chapter. Concerning further development of Montgomery's disagreements with Carl F.H. Henry specifically, see *Faith Founded On Fact*, Introduction, "Can Faith Rest On Fact?" xvii-xxv. My comments here are limited to the "Calvinists John Gerstner and R.C. Sproul, as well as Evangelical neo-Thomist Norman L. Geisler...."

It should be noted here, however, that Ronald Nash, Reformed Theological Seminary, Orlando, Florida branch, himself, though considered to be in the presuppositionalist camp, very cogently argues for the self-interpreting nature of historical facts: *Christian Faith and Historical Understanding*, esp. chapter six, "Historical Facts and Their Meaning," 93ff. Noteworthy is the 1984 copywrite on Nash's book, two years prior to Montgomery's *Human Rights & Human Dignity*. I (the author) personally interviewed Dr. Nash regarding his *Christian Faith and Historical Understanding*, especially chapter six.

evidence of a certain truth claim (say, Christ's claim to be God), *unless it can be established that the event comes in the context of a theistic universe.* For it makes no sense to claim to be the Son of God and to evidence it by an act of God (miracle) unless there is a God who can have a Son and who can act in a special way in the natural world. But in this case the mere fact of the resurrection cannot be used to establish the truth that there is a God. For the resurrection cannot even be a miracle unless there already is a God.[70]

Natural theology (i.e., "knowledge of God the creator") is able, according to Geisler, to demonstrate the existence of God.[71] The identity of Christ as the Son of God by his resurrection from the dead (cf. Rom. 1:4) then brings "knowledge of God the redeemer" (Special Revelation) to the world. Again, historical meaningfulness is imputed to this historical event because ours is a theistic universe. Without this presupposition (arrived at and verified *a posteriori*), the event loses its meaningfulness according to Geisler.

Further extension of Geisler's argument appears to bring us to the conclusion that if "an independent theistic structure" is not in place for the purpose of properly interpreting miraculous phenomena that take place within the purview of general historical events, then the interpretation of them is left to mere chance. But Montgomery's argument concerning the Resurrection, and the consequent inference of Christ's deity from that great historical event, is made evident by Jesus Himself:

---

70   Norman Geisler. *Christian Apologetics*. Grand Rapids: Baker, 1976. 95.

71   See R.C. Sproul, John Gerstner, Authur Lindsley. *Classical Apologetics*. Grand Rapids: Zondervan. 1984. 93-136 and Norman Geisler. *Christian Apologetics*. 237-259.

The classic argument from creation to the Creator is no where better presented than it was by the great historian of philosophy, F.C. Copleston, in his famous 1948 BBC debate with analytical philosopher, Bertrand Russell – See **Appendix One: "The Argument from Contingency."**

In my view there are two compelling reasons to accept Jesus' resurrection as implicating His deity, ... First, this miracle deals effectively with the most fundamental area of man's universal need, the conquest of death.... If death is indeed, that significant, then, "not to worship One who gives you the gift of eternal life is hopelessly to misread what the gift tells you about the Giver."[72]

Montgomery continues:

In the second place, there are logically only two possible kinds of explanation or interpretation of the fact of the Resurrection: that given by the person raised and that given by someone else. Surely, if only Jesus has been raised, He is in a far better position (indeed, in the **only** position!) to interpret or explain it.... And Jesus said His miraculous ministry is explicable because He was God in human form: "I and my Father are one"; "he who has seen me has seen the Father." Theism, then, becomes the proper inference from Jesus' resurrection as He Himself explained it — not a prior metaphysical hurdle to jump in order to arrive at a proper historical and evidential interpretation of that event.[73]

According to Professor Montgomery, a departure from a Christo-centric empirical method of historical investigation is simultaneously a departure from the possibility of historical objectivity.[74]

---

72 John W. Montgomery. *Faith Founded On Fact*. 61.

73 Montgomery. *Human Rights & Human Dignity*. 158-59.

74 The self-interpretation of historical facts is a critical factor *vis-à-vis* historical objectivity. Dr. Montgomery explains: "Were facts not self-interpreting, knowledge would be impossible, for the understanding of any given fact would require the understanding of another fact or facts, leading to infinite regress and the inability to explain the initial fact concerned." *Tractatus Logico-Theologicus*. 2.371. Montgomery continues: "If a fact or text is held not to have any inherent meaning, so that one must appeal beyond it to the interpreter for its true signification, then that must be true also for the extrinsic facts to which one appeals." Ibid. 2.3711. Further: "Bigger bugs have littler bugs upon their backs to bite 'em / And littler have littler bugs / And so — *ad infinitum*." Ibid. 2.3712. Conclusion: "Historians must regard facts as self-interpretating." Ibid. 2.372.

The consequences of this departure, according to Montgomery, are the draining of meaning from history and the consequent trivializing of the Gospel.[75]

WHERE IS HISTORY GOING?

Professor Montgomery inquires: "On what, then, does the case for Christianity rest? It rests, as the apostles well knew, on the objective, historical truth of the resurrection of Jesus Christ from the dead."[76] Since a systematic reconstruction of theological theorizing (Part 2) and the verification of the assertion: "When the historical facts of Christ's life, death, and resurrection are allowed to speak for themselves, they lead to belief in His deity and to acceptance of His account of the total historical process" (Part 3) follow, we need only to present Dr. Montgomery's outline of the Christian Worldview:

1. On the basis of accepted principles of textual and historical analysis, the Gospel records are found to be trustworthy historical documents — primary source evidence for the life of Christ.

2. In these records, Jesus exercises divine prerogatives and claims to be God in human flesh; and He rests His claims on His forthcoming resurrection.

3. In all four Gospels, Christ's bodily resurrection is described in minute detail; Christ's resurrection evidences His deity.

4. The fact of the resurrection cannot be discounted on *a priori*, philosophical grounds; miracles are impossible only if

---

75 Montgomery. *Where Is History Going?* 164.

76 "If Christ was not raised, then our gospel is null and void, and so is your faith" (1 Cor. 15:14). Throughout the book of Acts, the apostolic preaching again and again centers the truth of the Christian faith on the historical fact of the resurrection of Christ. Cf. Walter Künneth. "The Easter Message As the Essence of Theology." *Dialog*, I (Spring, 1962). 16-21. John Warwick Montgomery. *The Shape of the Past.* 138.

one so defines them — but such definition rules out proper historical investigation.[77]

5. If Christ is God, then He speaks the truth concerning the absolute divine authority of the Old Testament and of the soon-to-be-written New Testament; concerning His death for the sins of the world; and concerning the nature of man and of history.[78]

6. It follows from the preceding that all Biblical assertions bearing on philosophy of history are to be regarded as revealed truth, and that all human attempts at historical interpretation are to be judged for truth-value on the basis of harmony with Scriptural revelation.[79]

The Christian faith is founded upon historical fact and thus, historical Biblical Revelation constitutes the epistemological basis from which Christian experience and worship are given substantive conceptual meaningfulness. Part 2, "Theological Theory Formation" inquirers: Can theological models represent substantive-conceptual reality?

---

77 See Appendix Three: Biblical Miracles and Skepticism for development of this proposition.

78 See Appendix Five: The Unshakable Tradition of the Old Testament and Part Three: Verifying the Theological Model, Chapter Three: The Trustworthiness of the New Testament.

79 Ibid. 138-39. It should be observed that Montgomery's empirical methodology, as outlined above, follows after the Augustinian order of reasoning "from observable evidence (*scientia*) to faith in the person of Christ (or prophetic and apostolic spokesmen for God), and then to the invisible, eternal truths they reveal (*sapiential*). *Scientia* is prior to faith in alleged spokesmen for God, but faith in the Christ to whom they testify is prior to reception of God's redemptive plans and purposes (*sapiential*)"; Gordon R. Lewis. *Testing Christianity's Truth Claims*. Chicago: Moody Press, 1976. 68-69. Gordon Lewis's Ph.D. dissertation, "Faith and Reason in the Thought of St. Augustine," (Syracuse University, 1959) should be consulted for further development of Augustine's thoughts regarding his understanding of the inferential relation between *scientia* and *sapientia*.

PART 2:

THEOLOGICAL THEORY FORMATION

CHAPTER TWO

THEOLOGICAL MODELS AND SUBSTANTIVE-CONCEPTUAL REALITY

"The sense of the world must lie outside the world"[80]
— Ludwig Wittgenstein.

"In Negro legend, the devil meets his victim at a crossroad. Contemporary theology — and the church life which it so directly influences — stands at just such a crossroad, and the next step is fraught with tremendous peril."[81]

What is it to "do theology?" Numerous conflicting and inadequate answers (e.g., Bultmannian existentialism, the post-Bult-

---

80   Ludwig Wittgenstein. *Tractatus Logico-Philosophicus.* 6.41.

81   John Warwick Montgomery. *The Suicide of Christian Theology.* Minneapolis, MN: Bethany Fellowship Inc. 1970. 7.

mannian "New Hermeneutic" hold the field today; these have in common a basic misunderstanding as to the relation of theological theorizing to theory construction in other fields of knowledge, and a fundamental misconception in regard to the proper way of confirming or disconfirming theological judgments. In this essay a detailed comparison between scientific and theological methodologies is set forth, and the artistic and sacred dimensions of theological theorizing are explicated by way of an original structural model suggested by Wittgensteinian philosophical and linguistic analysis.[82]

How do we "do theology"? John W. Montgomery admonishes us to acknowledge that (1) the reductionism of contemporary theology is due to a "... basic misunderstanding as to the relation of theological theorizing to theory construction in other fields of knowledge..." and (2) these woefully inadequate methodologies (e.g., Bultmannian existentialism,[83] the post Bultmannian "New Hermeneutic"[84]) are marked by a "fundamental misconception in

---

82   Ibid. 267. Professor Montgomery's invitational paper, "The Theologians Craft: A Discussion of Theory Formation and Theory Testing in Theology," was presented August 24, 1965, at the 20th Annual Convention of the American Scientific Affiliation, convened at The King's College, Briarcliff Manor, New York. Montgomery's so-called "essay," the third word in the final sentence of the quote above, is here reused as part of the introduction of Chapter 2, of Part 2, in this book.

83   Christian existentialism is a theo-philosophical movement which takes an existentialist approach to Christian theology. That is, a "subjectivity of faith" rejects efforts to acknowledge God in an objective, logical system. To Kierkegaard, the focus of theology was on the individual grappling with subjective truth rather than a set of objective claims; a point he [Kierkegaard, 1813-1855] demonstrated by often writing under pseudonyms that had different points of view. He contended that each person must make independent choices, which then constitute his or her existence.

84   Bultmann believed that only a few scattered facts could be known about Jesus, and although a few things could be known about Jesus such a search was pointless for all that matters is following «the call of Jesus» which can only be known through an existential encounter with the word of God. And the "New hermeneutic" is the theory and methodology of interpretation to understand Biblical texts through existentialism. The essence of the new hermeneutic emphasizes not only the existence of language but also the fact that language is eventualized in the history of individual life. Bultmann relied on demythologization, an approach interpreting the mythological elements in the New Testament existentially. Bultmann contended that only faith in the kerygma, or proclamation, of the New Testament was necessary for Christian faith, not any particular facts regarding the historical Jesus. Bultmann's theological position, namely, that the Christian faith is, and should be, comparatively uninterested in the historical Jesus and centered instead on the transcendent Christ. Bultmann's theological position was shaped to a significant extent by Heidegger while they were colleagues at Marburg, Germany, 1922-28.

regard to the proper way of confirming or disconfirming theological judgments."

The existentialistic methodologies (primarily developed in the work of Karl Barth, Rudolph Bultmann, and Paul Tillich) fail to provide "an objective check on existential experience — in other words, a source of theological data outside of it, by which to judge it."[85] Montgomery comments on the devastating effects of the grave misconceptions of existentialistic methodologies:

> The foregoing criticisms, it is well to point out, also apply to those theologies which attempt to make a "living Christ" (as distinct from the Christ of Scripture) the source of theological theorizing. Such a "living Christ," if He is not known through Scripture, is necessarily known through extra-biblical experience. But, in the latter case, how can one be sure that his "Christ of experience" is the *real* Christ and not a projection of corporate religious needs and desires? The dangers of idolatry here are overwhelming.[86]

The *fait accompli* of non-propositional, existential theological methodologies is a "kerygmatic Christ," a mere mythical image in which the person and life of Jesus Christ is separated from historical fact, and which is subject to manipulation and shaping by the modern theologian's imagination. Consequently, a peculiarly private way of perceiving the Christian faith is required.[87]

Unfortunately for these positions, however, the analytical philosophy of the twentieth century has devastated attempts to "validate God-talk" by subjective faith experience on the ground

---

85   John Warwick Montgomery. *The Suicide of Christian Theology*. 283.

86   Ibid. 306.

87   For a thorough reading of Dr. Montgomery's penetrating critiques, of not only the works of Karl Barth, Rudolf Bultmann and Paul Tillich, but also a plethora of other scholars from the liberal and neo-orthodox theological traditions, see especially — *The Shape of the Past, Where Is History Going? Crisis In Lutheran Theology*, (Two Volumes) and *The Suicide of Christian Theology*.

that all pure subjectivities are in principle untestable. Their inner truth claims, being compatible with any and every state of affairs in the external world, are epistemologically meaningless.[88]

Professor Montgomery further comments on the consequences of the "epistemologically meaninglessness," i.e. anti-historical and anti-revelational ideological views of holy Scripture, that hold sway over the contemporary conceptual and linguistic crisis in theology:

> A favorite preacher's text is 1 Corinthians 14:8: "If the trumpet gives an uncertain sound, who shall prepare himself to the battle?" Those who quote the verse perceive that the contemporary church suffers from uncertainty as to its message. The problem, however, is a good deal more acute. In large regions of the ecclesiastical landscape, the warriors appear totally incapable of identifying the battle-lines. The silence is ominous: hardly anyone seems to be able to find the trumpet, much less to play even uncertain sounds on it.[89]

Theology, in the thinking of many contemporary theologians and preachers alike, does not refer to reality but is merely silence qualified by parables and symbols.[90] Consequently, the public, yet

---

88 John Warwick Montgomery. *Faith Founded On Fact*. 46.
   For further consideration of the philosophical controversy surrounding the issue of the validity of "God talk," Professor Montgomery notes: "See especially Kai Nielson, 'Can Faith Validate God-Talk?' *New Theology No. 1*, ed. Martin Marty and Dean Peerman, New York: Macmillan Paperbacks, 1964, Ch. 8, 94-104, and C.B. Martin, 'A Religious Way of Knowing,' *New Essays in Philosophical Theology*. Edited by Antony Flew and Alasdair MacIntyre. London: SCM Press, 1955."

89 _____. "Biblical Inerrancy: What Is At Stake." *God's Inerrant Word: An International Symposium On The Trustworthiness of Scripture*. Edited by John Warwick Montgomery. 15.

90 Cambridge University's Herbert Butterfield penetrates to the heart of the modern theological crisis: "It would be a dangerous error to imagine that the characteristics of an historical religion would be maintained if the Christ of the theologians were divorced from the Jesus of history." *Christianity and History*. London: Collins Fontana Books. 1957. 168. Dr. Montgomery agrees with Butterfield: "History can be removed from Christian theology only by the total destruction of theology itself." *Where Is History Going?* 112.

seemingly faint trumpets of evangelical theological methodologies, have become increasingly marginalized in our present day.[91]

What is the proper way, according to Montgomery, "of confirming or disconfirming theological judgments"? Positively, the relating of theological theorizing to theory construction in other fields of knowledge involves the rigorous application of an empirical theological method.[92] Demonstration of empirical method involves a "...detailed comparison between scientific and theological methodologies..." providing for the epistemic justification of Christian experience and worship qua a divinely inspired, inerrant Bible's "epistemological vividness," i.e., the validation of "God-talk" (contrary to the "epistemologically meaningless" fate of existential methodologies).

Theological theorizing begins at the level of the scientific. The scientific level of theological theorizing engages the objective empirical world. God's personal self-disclosure, i.e., Biblical Revelation, flows through the union of ordinary history (*historie*) and *heilsgeschichte* (salvation-history), to mankind. Biblical Revelation constitutes the epistemological source from which Christian experience and worship are given meaningfulness.

The artistic and the sacral dimensions of theological theorizing (both are explained below) are then "explicated by way of an original structural model suggested by Wittgensteinian philosophical and linguistic analysis" (i.e., the artistic and sacral dimensions of theological theorizing are added to the scientific *via* a Christo-centric, empirical method).

Theology involves a "speaking-of-God"; however, the double meaning standing behind this expression must not go unacknowledged: "theology speaks *about* God (the objective genitive of the

---

91   The critical thinking reader will observe that "our present day" persists to the time I am presently writing, 2025.

92   John Warwick Montgomery. *The Shape of the Past.* 138.

grammarians), but only because of 'God's speaking to man' (the subjective genitive) ...."[93]

A more thorough development of scientific theory formation and testing followed by a comparison of scientific and theological theorizing, will serve the purpose of further demonstrating the proper way, according to Montgomery, of confirming or disconfirming theological assertions.

THEOLOGICAL THEORIZING — THE NATURE OF SCIENTIFIC THEORY

What is the nature of scientific theory? Although the nature of scientific theory varies, common theoretical denominators are not difficult to discover. For example, Professor Montgomery points to Wittgenstein's analogy of the Net: "Theories are nets cast to catch what we call the 'the world': to rationalize, to explain, and to master it. We endeavor to make the mesh ever finer and finer."[94] Harvard's Leonard Nash adds: "He who realizes the existence of such a conceptual fabric, and is capable of lifting it, carries with it all its cords, all the colligative relations it accommodates."[95]

---

93   Montgomery. *The Suicide of Christian Theology.* The scientific, artistic, and sacral levels of theological theorizing in Montgomery's thought corresponds with Luther's three stipulations for adequacy in theological work., "Meditatio," "Tentatio," and "Oratio." Dr. Montgomery notes: "This passage appears in the Preface to the German section of the first edition of Luther's collected writings (Wittgenberg, 1539). For an excellent discussion of it, see Piper. *Christian Dogmatics.* Translated and edited by T. Engelder, J.T. Mueller, and W.W.F. Abreacht, 4 vols. St. Louis, MO.: Concordia, 1950-1957. I, 186-90." In John Warwick Montgomery. Ibid. 299 & 309. "Meditatio" in Luther's thought, relates to the objective, historical side of the Christian faith and involves the reading, studying and contemplation of the Scriptures. "Tentatio" refers to subjective, experiential involvement, and by "Oratio" the Reformer is referring to prayer, that dimension of theological theorizing wherein the theologian experiences communion with the Holy One.

    Luther's model may be compared with the Reformed model of faith used in classical Protestant orthodoxy which begins with "Notitia," referring to objective, scientific knowledge followed by "Assensus," referring to intellectual assent as the subjective embrace of the faith and "Fiducia," which involves trust as part of one's regenerating relationship with God.

94   Ibid. 272. Karl R. Popper, *The Logic of Scientific Discovery.* 2d ed. London: Hutchinson, 1959. 59. For Wittgenstein's presentation of the "net" analogy, see *Tractatus Logio-Philosophicus.* 6.341-6.35.

95   Leonard Nash. *The Nature of the Natural Sciences.* Boston, MA: Little, Brown, 1963. 61. In John Warwick Montgomery. *The Suicide of Christian Theology.* 272.

Professor Montgomery observes that "The use of an image (the net) to illustrate the nature of scientific theory construction points to an especially vital element in such theories: the employ-ment of 'models' — representations that carry 'epistemological vividness.'"[96] Scientific theory formation, understood in terms of the "Net" analogy, involves the relating of existent empirical facts properly, i.e., theoretical formation involves an attempt to prop-erly *fit the facts*. Thus, the "theory maker must never suppose that he is building reality; his task is the fascinating but more humble one of shaping a 'conceptual fabric' that, with 'epistemological vividness,' will correctly mirror the world of substantive reality."[97]

It must be stressed that scientific theories, contrary to deduc-tive argument from experimental data alone or the logic-book type of induction employed by philosophers, or indeed, any other for-mal method, bring deduction and induction into a more comple-mentary relationship. One of Montgomery's mentors at Cornell, Max Black, insists we should "think of science as a concrescence, a growing together of variable, interacting, mutually reinforcing factors contributing to a development organic in character."[98]

---

96   Ibid. Frederick Ferre' notes that models can provide cognitivity and truth concerning religious language. Ferre' defines model as that "which provides epistemological vividness or immediacy to theory by offering as an interpretation... something that both fits the logical form of the theory and is well-known...." Scope is concerned with the model's degree of inclusiveness, i.e., how much reality does it purport to reflect, and the model's status points to its importance in terms of its dispensability or indispensability. Frederick Ferre'. *Basic Modern Philosophy of Religion*. New York: Schribner, 1967. 373f., and "Mapping the Logic of Models in Science and Theology." *The Christian Scholar*. XLVI. Spring 1963. 13f.

97   *The Suicide of Christian Theology*. 273. Montgomery carefully observes: "Of course, theories can themselves become the substantive grist for the mill of higher-level theory, but this in no way lessens the need to distinguish sharply between that which is to be explained (*explicandum*) and that which does the explaining (*explicans*). 302.

98   Max Black. "The Definition of Scientific Method." In Black's: *Problems of Analysis: Philosophical Essays*. London: Routledge & Kegan Paul. 1954. 23. John Warwick Montgomery. Ibid. 274.

Leonard Nash illustrates the generation of scientific knowledge in the following diagram:[99]

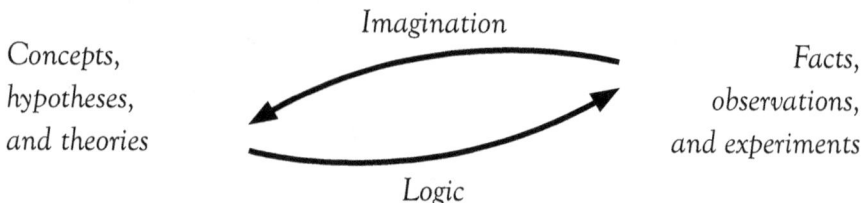

Imagination

Concepts, hypotheses, and theories

Facts, observations, and experiments

Logic

Scientific theory formation, as illustrated above, involves "imagination." Professor Montgomery explains:

> The essential place of "imagination" in scientific theorizing has been greatly stressed by Einstein; and its role can perhaps best be seen by introducing, alongside induction and deduction — as, in fact, the connecting link between — Peirce's concept of "retroduction" or "abduction," based on Aristotle's ἀπαγωγή type inference.[100] "Abduction," writes Peirce, "consists in studying facts and devising a theory to explain them.... Deduction proves that something *must* be; Induction shows that something *actually is* operative; Abduction merely suggests something *may be*."[101]

Montgomery asserts: "It is particularly important to note that the validity of a scientific theory depends squarely upon its applicability as a conceptual Gestalt; experimental confirmation through predictive success is of secondary importance and is of-

---

99   Ibid. John Warwick Montgomery. 274.

100   Aristotle. *Prior Analytics*. ii. 25. Cf. *Posterior Analytics*. ii. 19.

101   C.S. Peirce. *Collected Papers*. Harvard ed. V, para. 146. 171. In John Warwick Montgomery. *Suicide of Christian Theology*. 274. Montgomery cautions: "It should go without saying that acceptance of the Peirce-Aristotle retroduction concept in no way commits one to Peirce's pragmatic philosophy; I myself have argued strongly against pragmatic epistemologies in my book, *The Shape of the Past: An Introduction to Philosophical Historiography*. ("History in Christian Perspective." I. Ann Arbor, MI.: Edwards Brothers. 1963. 320-29. Ibid. 302.

ten of necessity, dispensed with entirely."[102] Therefore, we conclude that theories are attempts to develop patterns in which data will appear intelligible. Professor Montgomery appeals to N.R. Hanson for further development of this point:

> A theory is not pieced together from observed phenomena; it is rather what makes it possible to observe phenomena as being of a certain sort, and as related to other phenomena. Theories put phenomena into systems. They are built up in "reverse" — retroductively. A theory is a cluster of conclusions in search of a premise. From the observed properties of phenomena, the physicist reasons his way towards a keystone idea from which the properties are explicable as a matter of course.[103]

Professor Montgomery's summary point is that the retroductive transmission of data into intelligible patterns (Gestalts) produces theories that constitute a "keystone idea" from which scientific models are constructed. This thought will serve to introduce the relation between theological theorizing and model construction to scientific formation and testing.

THEOLOGICAL THEORIZING — VERIFICATION AND FALSIFICATION

"Is not theology a unique realm of the 'spirit,' unscientific by its very nature?"[104] Indeed, the modern estrangement of theology from historical, empirical facticity, producing a non-factual, non-testable foundation for the Christian faith, has driven many non-Christians to conclude that theological assertions are mean-

---

102   Ibid. 276.

103   N.R. Hanson. *Patterns of Discovery: An Inquiry into the Conceptual Foundations of Science.* Cambridge University Press. 1958. 87-90. In John Warwick Montgomery. Ibid. 275.

104   John Warwick Montgomery. *The Suicide of Christian Theology.* 276.

ingless. Professor Montgomery points to the non-Christian perception of the Christian faith through a presentation of Antony Flew's parable, developed from a tale told by John Wisdom:

Once upon a time two explorers came upon a clearing in the jungle. In the clearing were growing many flowers and many weeds. One explorer says, "Some gardener must tend this plot." The other disagrees, "there is no gardener." So, they pitch their tents and set a watch. No gardener is ever seen. "But perhaps he is an invisible gardener." So, they set up a barbed-wire fence. They electrify it. They patrol with bloodhounds. (For they remember how H.G. Wells' *The Invisible Man* could be both smelt and touched though he could not be seen.) But no shrieks ever suggest that some intruder has received a shock. No movements of the wire ever betray an invisible climber. The bloodhounds never give cry. Yet still the Believer is not convinced. "But there is a gardener, invisible, insensible to electric shocks, a gardener who comes secretly to look after the garden which he loves." At last, the Sceptic despairs, "But what remains of your original assertion? Just how does what you call an invisible, intangible, eternally elusive gardener differ from an imaginary gardener or even from no gardener at all?"[105]

Indeed, this parable is condemning to both modern ideological approaches to the Christian faith and all world religions with self-evident, *aprioristic* starting points. Why? The answer lies in the fact that their presuppositions are insulated within the domain of the individual believer's personal experience and consequently, they are removed from objective testing and the corresponding possibility of verification or falsification. Montgomery, however,

---

105 Antony Flew. "Theology and Falsification." *New Essays in Philosophical Theology*. Edited by Antony Flew and Alasdair MacIntyre. London: SCM Press, 1955. 96. In John Warwick Montgomery. *Faith Founded On Fact*. 40-41.

strenuously contends *in extenso* that this is not the case with historic Christianity:

> ... Christianity is unique in claiming intrinsic, not merely extrinsic, connection with the empirical reality which is the subject of scientific investigation. Christianity is a *historical* religion — historical in the very special sense that its entire revelational content is wedded to historical manifestations of Divine power. The pivot of Christian theology is the biblical affirmation that ὁ λόγος σὰρξ ἐγένετο (John 1:14): God Himself came to earth — entered man's empirical sphere — in Jesus Christ, and the revelation of God in the history of Israel served as a pointer to Messiah's coming, and His revelation in the Apostolic community displayed the power of Christ's Spirit.[106] From the first verse of the Bible to the last God's *contact* with man's world is affirmed. And throughout Scripture human testimony to objective, empirical encounter with God is presented in the strongest terms.[107] Christian theology thus has no fear of scientific, empirical investigation; quite the contrary, the historical nature of the Christian faith — as distinguished from the subjective, existential character of

---

106   Dr. Montgomery states: "I made this point *in extenso* in the apologetic lectures I delivered at the University of British Columbia on January 29 and 30, 1963; these have been published in a slightly abridged version as a series of four articles under the general title "History and Christianity," and *His*, December, 1964 — March, 1965; the lectures are now available in original form in my *Where Is History Going?* Grand Rapids, MI: Zondervan, 1969. chaps. ii-iii.

107   To King Agrippa Paul thus defended the empirical facticity of Christ's fulfillment of prophecy and resurrection: "I am speaking the sober truth. For the king knows about these things, and to him I speak freely; for I am persuaded that none of these things has escaped his notice, for this was not done in a corner" (Acts 26:25-26). Peter's Pentecost sermon contains the significant lines: "Men of Israel, hear these words: Jesus of Nazareth, a man attested to you by God with mighty works and wonders and signs which God did through him in your midst, as you yourselves know..." (Acts 2:22; cf. F.F. Bruce. *The New Testament Documents: Are They Reliable?* 5th ed.: London: InterVarsity Fellowship. 1960. 45-46.

the other world religions[108] — demands objective, scientific theologizing.[109]

The Christian *defensio fidei* begins with "... heuristic, methodological presuppositions that permit us to discover what the world is like — and (equally important) what it is not like. Such are the *aprioris* of empirical method, which are not only heuristic but 'unavoidably necessary' in all of our endeavors to distinguish synthetic truth from falsity."[110] Simply put, historic Christianity contends that the *Gardener* has *actually* entered the *Garden* in space-time and ordinary history. And therefore, the life, death and resurrection of Christianity's Founder, Jesus of Nazareth, is open to either empirical verification of falsification. Beyond the limits of empirical research, we may properly infer the Numinous in theological theory formation. Dr. Montgomery comments on the inferential bond between science and Christianity:

> The theological theorist, like his scientific counterpart, will endeavor to formulate conceptual Gestalts — "networks" of ideas capable of rendering his data intelligible. He will employ "models" to achieve epistemological vividness. He will utilize all three types of inference (inductive,

---

108 Professor Montgomery notes: "It might seem that such a general statement would not apply to Islam; however, see my article, "The Apologetic Approach of Muhammed Ali and Its Implications for Christian Apologetics. *Muslim World.* LI. April 1961. 111-22. (See author's 'Corrigendum' in the July 1961 *Muslim World.* No world religion other than Christianity stakes its life on the objective historic facticity of its claims; only the Christian faith dares to make such an assertion as Paul's: 'If Christ has not been raised, then our preaching is in vain and your faith is in vain'" (1 Cor. 15:14).

109 Montgomery. *The Suicide of Christian Theology.* 277.

110 Montgomery. *Where Is History Going?* 179. Although all arguments begin with *a prioris*, this need not present a presuppositional obstacle to the seeker after substantive, objective truth. Professor Montgomery observes:

Strictly speaking, all apologetic arguments are rational in type, for Kant has shown that philosophical presuppositions precede all forms of empirical inquiry. However, the *a prioris* of empirical investigation (to be distinguished sharply from those of logical positivism) are of a simple, self-evident variety, and instead of precluding discovery and intellectual progress, seem to provide valuable tools for investigative activity. Therefore, it appears wise to retain the distinction between rational and empirical arguments — a distinction incidentally, which is fundamental in understanding the role and development of modern science. *Faith Founded On Fact.* 92-93.

deductive, retroductive) in his theory making, but, again like the scientist, he will find himself most usually dependent upon the imaginative operation of retroduction.[111]

Science and Christianity alike "generally proceed retroductively, and neither is less concerned than the other about the concrete verification of its inferences."[112] The coherent *fitting of the facts* is important to both historic Christianity and modern scientific theorizing. This most significant point leads to Montgomery's conclusion that at the scientific level of theological theorizing, the empirical net of Christianity uniquely qualifies it as "the only religion which purports to offer external, objective evidence of its validity. All other religions appeal to inner experience without any means of objective validation."[113]

How does one construct the scientific or theological model? What data does the scientist or theologian attempt to fit? Professor Montgomery's observations provide incisive answers:

> In science, ... the irreducible stuff which theorizing attempts to grasp in its net is the natural world, and this includes every phenomenal manifestation in the universe. Science knows no investigative boundaries; its limits are imposed not by the stuff with which it is permitted to deal, but by the manner in which it can treat data. *Ex hypothesi,* science is methodologically capable of studying the world in an *objective* manner only: it can examine anything that touches human experience, but it can never, qua science, "get inside" its subject matter; it always stands outside and describes. This is, of course, both the glory and the pathos of science: it can analyze everything but is prevented from experiencing the heart of anything. On the objective, sci-

---

111 Montgomery. *The Suicide of Christian Theology.* 277.
112 Ibid. 278.
113 John Warwick Montgomery. *The Shape of the Past.* 140.

entific level, however, theology has no greater advantage; it likewise stands outside its data and analyzes.[114]

And precisely what does theology analyze at the scientific level? Through the employment of conceptual Gestalts, the theologian attempts to render intelligible the data of "revelational experience": "Theological theories endeavor to 'fit the facts' of such experience; theology on this level is thus one segment of scientific activity as a whole — that segment concerned with revelational, as opposed to non-revelational, phenomena."[115]

The ambiguity created by the term "revelational experience" brings the theologian to a fork in the road and he is cautioned concerning his next step, "since a false step here will tragically weaken the entire process of theological theorizing — either by emasculation (if one excludes from purview genuine revelational data), or by adulteration (if one mixes non-revelational considerations with the truly revelational subject matter). And, ironically, it is exactly at this point that Christian theology has all too often trumpeted forth an uncertain sound — or, worse, a positive discord!"[116] These thoughts bring Montgomery to a methodological crossroad; instead of the peculiarly private notes of many modern theological trumpets — i.e., existential methodologies — the now faint notes of *Sola Scriptura* must again be loudly trumpeted!

CHRISTIAN EPISTEMOLOGY: THE BIBLE

"Through Christian history, the 'revelational experience' which yields the proper data for theological theorizing has been understood as having either a *single* source or *multiple* sources."[117]

---

114 Montgomery. *The Suicide of Christian Theology*. 279.
115 Ibid.
116 Ibid. 280.
117 Ibid.

Multiple source traditions, e.g., Roman Catholicism, Greek Orthodoxy, Anglo-Catholicism (all holding to the belief of the equal epistemological footing of church tradition and the Bible) and numerous pseudo-Christian cults, e.g., Mormonism and its *Book of Mormon* or Christian Science and Mary Baker Eddy's *Science and Health,* as co-authorities with the Bible and, as well, many modern Protestant theological perspectives that attribute equal authority to biblical insight, church teaching and personal experience all share a common fallacy:

> All multiple-source views of the subject matter of theology are, however, unstable. They tend to give preference to one source rather than to another, or to seek some single, more fundamental source lying behind the multiple sources already accepted. Among the sects, the Bible has been virtually swallowed up by whatever special "sacred book" has been put alongside of it;[118] tradition has been more determinative than biblical teaching in the theological development of Greek Orthodoxy and Roman Catholicism; and the "New Hermeneutic" seems incapable of withstanding the old Bultmannian gravitational pull away from the biblical text toward the other dialectic pole of contemporary existential interpretation. In the "New Shape" Roman Catholicism of Karl Rahner, Kung, *et al.,* a conscious attempt is being made to get behind the dualism of scripture and tradition through affirming a unity of "Holy Writ *and* Holy Church";[119] yet such dialectic, like that of the Protestant "New Hermeneutic,"[120] does not escape the charge

---

118 See Walter R. Martin's classic work: *The Kingdom of the Cults.* Minneapolis, MN: Bethany House Publishers. Revised and expanded, 1985.

119 Dr. Montgomery notes: "On this trend, see especially George H. Tavard, who argues that 'the authority of the Church's tradition and that of Scripture are not two, but one." *Holy Writ or Holy Church.* New York: Harper, 1959. 244. Montgomery. *The Suicide of Christian Theology.* 305.

120 Ernst Kasemann. "Essays on New Testament Themes." *Studies in Biblical Theology.* No. 41. London: SCM Press, 1964. 58, is representative of the "New Hermeneutic" in his comments: In New Testament language we are driven to test the spirits even within Scripture itself. We cannot simply

of question-begging. This is the essential, insurmountable difficulty in all multiple-source approaches to theological theorizing. They leave unanswered the question of *final* authority. What do we do as Roman Catholics when Holy Writ and Holy Church *disagree?* What do we do as Tillichians when church history, the Bible and history of culture are not in accord?[121] Obviously, one must either frankly admit that one source is final or establish a criterion of judgment over all previously accepted sources — which criterion becomes, *ex hypothesi,* the final source! Multiple source approaches to the subject matter of theology thus logically — whether one likes it or not — reduce to single source interpretations.[122]

---

accept a dogma or a system of doctrine but are placed in a situation *vis-a-vis Scripture* which is, at the same time and inseparably, both responsibility and freedom. Only to such an attitude can the Word of God reveal itself in Scripture; and that Word, as biblical criticism makes plain, has no existence in the realm of the objective — that is, outside our act of decision."

121 Professor Montgomery's thoughts here include Paul Tillich's understanding of the historical drama as, first in terms of man's essential union with God followed by the existential conditions of life conceived by the nonhistorical symbol of the fall, and back to the essentialization of man's participation in the "New Being." Tillich develops a dialectic, i.e., the concepts of heteronomy-autonomy-theonomy, *vis-à-vis* his understanding and interpretation of history. Dr. Montgomery provides succinct definition of these concepts in stating that, "By 'heteronomy' Tillich means the imposition of law upon man from outside himself; by 'autonomy,' man's attempt to make his own laws and determine his own fate, and by 'theonomy,' the rule God's law, which calls man to be what he was meant to be. (*The Shape of the Past.* 128). The three terms, heteronomy, autonomy and theonomy, derive from the Greek: "law of another" (heteronomy), "law of oneself" (autonomy), and "divine law" (theonomy).

122 Montgomery. *The Suicide of Christian Theology.* 281. Professor Montgomery's comments, *Where Is History Going?* Appendix E. 240-241. GOD PLUS THREE: A Review of *History: Written and Lived.* By Paul Weiss. Southern Illinois University Press, 1962. 245 pages, are noteworthy here:

As W.N. Clark well noted in his comments on Wiess's *Mode of Being,* the Weissian System "leaves untouched the ...fundamental and, for a metaphysician, unavoidable problem of the ultimate origin or source of existence and the ultimate principle of unity of this whole with its four irreducible modes", (*Yale Review,* Sept. 1958). Moreover, since Weiss regards systematic philosophy much as Barth, Tillich, and Bultmann regard systematic theology — as a circular enterprise in which epistemology grounds ontology and ontology grounds epistemology — his total system, to use Morris Weitz's expression, lacks "testability" (*Ethics,* October 1961).

Montgomery's *The Shape of the Past,* demonstrates the meaning of history (which shapes the meaning of life itself) through contending that man must receive an objectively reliable Revelation originating from the human situation. Without God's Revelation of Himself in Jesus Christ, mankind is hopelessly in the dark as to the meaning of the past. See also Montgomery's very intriguing work, *Principalities and Powers,* Minneapolis: Bethany House Publishers, 1973, especially pages 43-46 for comments related to this subject.

Multiple-source fallacies, *vis-à-vis* religious authority, e.g., Reason and Scripture (eighteenth-century "Enlightenment" Liberal tradition), Church and Scripture (Greek Orthodoxy and Roman Catholicism) or Experience and Scripture (Schleiermacher-Ritschl-Fosdick era through Bultmannian existentialism and beyond) all invariably share the common dilemma of having to choose between competing authorities at the inevitable point of disagreement between the varied authorities. "What is clearly needed is an objective check on existential experience — in other words, a source of theological data outside of it, by which to judge it.... Thus, we arrive at the Bible — the source by which Reason, Church, and Religious Experience can and must be evaluated theologically. We reach this point not simply by process of elimination, but more especially because only Scripture can be validated as a genuine source of theological truth."[123]

Professor Montgomery's contention that Biblical Revelation must be the sole source of truth for theological theorizing raises very serious questions: "Specifically, (1) Is the Bible an inerrantly reliable source of revelational data? (2) Is the Bible self-interpreting? (3) Does the Bible provide the norms as well as the subject matter for theological theory construction?"[124]

Doctrinal debates in any age, e.g., Patristic, Medieval, Reformation down to the present, must ultimately be decided by an objective, infallible standard of truth.[125] Montgomery qualifies his contention that the Bible must be regarded as the only source for theological data by laying great stress on the non-separation of inspiration and inerrancy: "Note carefully that I have not said merely (as others have said) that inspiration and inerrancy *should* not be separated (i.e., that they *can* be separated but for various biblical and theological reasons *ought* not to be), but rather that

---

123   Ibid. 283.
124   Ibid. 284.
125   John Warwick Montgomery. *Crisis In Lutheran Theology.* Vol. I, 15-16.

scriptural inspiration and inerrancy *cannot* exist apart from each other (i.e., that to separate them results not just in error, but in plain simple *meaninglessness*)."[126]

Contemporary oppositions to inerrancy are *not* founded upon *empirical evidence*; they are rather rooted in *a priori* philosophical commitments: "That is to say, there has been an alteration in the philosophical Zeitgeist which, apart from the question of particular factual evidence, makes scriptural inerrancy offensive to much of contemporary theological thought."[127]

Professor Montgomery properly identifies the speculative nature of contemporary attacks on biblical inerrancy as "nonsensical" — that is, they are lacking criteria necessary for verification:

> The importance of the analytic approach to questions of truth and falsity cannot be overestimated. As a result of its application, vast areas of philosophical speculation and argument have been shown to be in a never-never land of meaninglessness — a land where discussion could continue forever without any possibility of arriving at truth or falsity. The analysts have successfully cleared the philosophical air of numerous positions about which discussion of truth-value is a waste of time, because their verifiability is impossible in any case.[128]

---

126 Ibid. 18.

127 Ibid. 21.

128 Ibid. 27. If a position, in principle, cannot be verified or falsified, then that position is meaningless because no proper interpretation can be applied to the position in question. All interpretations of any position that cannot be verified or falsified, must be positivistic, i.e., interpretations reduce to arbitrary meaninglessness. The nature of the criterion used for the interpretation of philosophical verifiability is discussed by Professor Montgomery (Ibid. footnote #30):

Attempts have been made, of course, to destroy the Verifiability Criterion. Few traditional, speculative philosophers, have been happy with Feigl's remark that "Philosophy is the disease of which analysis should be the cure!" But the Verifiability Principle still stands as the best available road map through the forest of truth-claims. One of the most persistent attempts to refute the Criterion has been the effort to show that it is itself a meaningless assertion, being evidently neither an analytic nor a synthetic statement. However, this objection has been effectively met both by Ayer, who argues that the Criterion is actually a definition (*Language, Truth and Logic.* New York: Dover Publications, 1946. 15-16) and by Hempel, who shows that it, "like the result of any other explication, represents a linguistic proposal which itself is neither true nor false" (The Empiricist

The philosophical air of contemporary theological oppositions to inerrancy has been polluted in a threefold manner: "It is
alleged, first, that the gospel and the spiritual content of the Bible
can be affirmed without regarding the Scripture as inerrant; sec-
ondly, that Christ can be adequately preached without Scripture
being inerrant; and thirdly, that one can sensibly affirm the infallibility of the Bible even though one does not agree to the veracity
of all of its details."[129]

Professor Montgomery explains the first of the contemporary
allegations against biblical inerrancy:

1. *Inerrant gospel without inerrant Scripture?* One of the
   most basic convictions of the non-inerrancy position
   on Scripture is that its theological, and moral content
   can be unqualifiedly relied upon even though its historical, scientific, and other nontheological assertions
   reflect the fallible knowledge of the biblical writers'
   own time. Since the Bible was given by God for the
   salvation of men, it is argued that only the salvatory
   content of Scripture is consequential theologically,
   and nothing is lost if the Bible turns out to be fallible when it deals with matters irrelevant to redemptive
   truth and morality.[130]

This position is analytically meaningless.[131] Why? Because, in
principle, the salvatory (theological) statements, representative of
the Gospel, cannot be verified or falsified. Why trust in Christian theological assertions that are, by their very nature, removed

---

Criterion of Meaning," published originally in the *Revue Internationale de Philosophie*, IV, 1950,
and reprinted, with newly appended remarks by the author, in *Logical Positivism*, ed. A.J. Ayer.
Glencoe, Illinois: Free Press, 1959. 108-129.

129   John Warwick Montgomery. "Biblical Inerrancy: What Is a Stake?" *God's Inerrant Word: An International Symposium On The Trustworthiness Of Scripture.* Ed. By John Warwick Montgomery. 23.

130   Ibid. 23-24.

131   Ibid. 25-26.

to the relative hidden domain of individual personal experience instead of trusting in the variety of other proposed religious experiences by competing world religions and cults?

The second of the contemporary attacks on an inerrant view of Scripture is introduced by Professor Montgomery:

> 2. *A saving Christ without an inerrant Scripture?* Since it is the living Christ who saves and not a book, liberal evangelicals consider axiomatic the conviction that an errant Bible is powerless to detract from the heart of Christianity. Jesus will still be the same, yesterday, today and forever: still as much capable of saving men as He ever was. An evangelical is one who preaches the "evangel," and the evangel is Christ — so why should a good evangelical have to do more that preach Christ? Is not the inerrancy of Scripture an albatross about the neck, reducing the Christian's effectiveness in evangelism by forcing him to defend Scripture when he should simply be proclaiming God's love in Christ?[132]

The saving acts of Christ, upon which the proclamation of the Gospel depends, were as much historical as theological.

> Thus, an errancy view of Scripture relative to its alleged "secular" contents will as thoroughly undermine the portrait of Jesus as it will the general theological or moral teachings of the Bible or the biblical gospel. Indeed, since few would dispute that the theological, ethical, and evangelical content of Scripture came to particular focus in Jesus' earthly ministry, the reliability of the biblical message of salvation is directly bound up with the historical reliability of that ministry. There is no avoiding the issue of the "secular" veracity of Scripture in the interests of

---

132 Ibid. 28.

the "spiritual": and certainly not in the life of the biblical Savior, whose miraculous birth took place in the days of Herod the King and whose death and resurrection occurred under Pontius Pilate.[133]

The last of the non-inerrant views addressed by Montgomery seemingly requires an implicit, esoteric kind of insight:

3. *An infallible Bible in spite of errors?* Sensing the uncomfortable implications of a partial inerrancy view that would focus only on the gospel or Jesus in Scripture, liberal evangelicals endeavor, as we have already observed, to hold to plenary inspiration while at the same time admitting to *de facto* biblical error. This is generally accomplished by claiming (a) that the Bible is always — plenarily — true in its divine intent, but (b) it does not necessarily intend to convey factually true information in non-revelatory matters.[134]

Revelation, according to this position, is not inscripturated and is essentially unverifiable apart from the individual eye and/ or ear of faith.[135] Professor Montgomery exposes the logical weaknesses of this third opposition to inerrancy:

Two crushing logical fallacies characterize this argumentation, one relating to the problem of "intent" (the intentional fallacy) and the other to the over-all meaningfulness of the claim to intentional reliability (technical nonsensicality).

---

133 Ibid. Also see, John Warwick Montgomery. *Crisis In Lutheran Theology.* Vol., I, 26-27 for further discussion of the need of verifiability.

134 Ibid. 29.

135 In the 1965 Duquesne volume, Albert C. Outler and Markus Barth clearly represent this errant position: "It is unwise in any form whatsoever to speak of he 'absolute authority of the Bible.' For the Bible is no wise an absolute... It is relative to the Holy Spirit." John Warwick Montgomery. *Ecumenicity, Evangelicals, and Rome.* Grand Rapids, MI: Zondervan, 1969. Footnotes, 38 and 39.

Professor Montgomery defines, *in extenso*, these two logical fallacies as they relate to our present discussion:

> ... the totality of any creative or didactic work is the only proper basis for understanding it. Since "the material and the medium have their own powers of expression," one cannot isolate an alleged intention of the author by which to create value-levels in his work ("revelational," "non-revelational"). Obviously, he intended to put everything in his work that is there, or it would not be there; obviously also he intended (if he is a truthful person) to convey no falsehoods and to be as accurate as possible. Neither the human authors nor the divine Author of Scripture intended to do other than they did in writing the Bible; or, putting it more explicitly, if they did intend something else, we would have no way of knowing it. The work itself — the entire biblical text — is our only basis for saying anything about the author's intent. Presumably, in the issue of inerrancy, the prime concern is with the supervening "intent" of the divine Author, and the incarnate Christ tells us simply, quoting the God of the Old Testament, that "man shall not live by bread alone, but by *every word* that proceedeth out of the mouth of God." One must therefore operate with every word and consider every word as significant. Had God "intended" otherwise, the text would (by definition) be different from what it is![136]

---

136 Ibid. 31. On page 41, endnote #34, Montgomery further discusses the intentional fallacy:
The intentional fallacy, it should be carefully noted, does *not* apply to the inductive determination of an author's purpose by the examination of the word he has written; such efforts to derive the larger or lesser purposes of composition are part and parcel of all responsible interpretation of literature, written creative or didactic. One commits the intentional fallacy, rather, when one performs either or both of the following operations: (1) the author's alleged intent is derived *extrinsically* — from outside the work to be interpreted — and is then forced on the work regardless of the natural meaning of the work taken by itself; and (2) the author's alleged intent, obtained either from outside his composition or even within the composition, is employed as a *reductionistic principle* for discounting what he has in fact said in his work or the truth-value of it. In short, one can and should try to learn an author's purpose in writing, but this must be learned through analysis of his composition itself, and must not be used as a critical principle to evacuate his work

Is it necessary to assume that merely because God says something, it must be true? Possibly Christ was subject to human ideas and cultural restraints. If this were the case, then how could we trust in his view of Scripture?

The first of these arguments is reflected in Descartes's discussion of God as a possible "Evil Genius" — a cosmic liar. But if He were, He would be a divine and, therefore, consummate liar, so you would be incapable of catching Him at it. In short, He would be a better liar than you are a detective. So, the very idea of God as liar is meaningless — an analytically unverifiable notion in principle. Once you have met God incarnate, you have no choice but to trust Him: as to the way of salvation, as the reliability of the entire Bible, and as to human rights.[137]

Dualistic positions regarding Scripture eliminate themselves *a priori*. The separating of Christ from history ends in an intellectual and spiritual vacuum. Contemporary Christians must not "sell their biblical heritage for a mess of outdated philosophical pottage. In the Bible and in the Christ to whom it testifies God

---

of its substantive content. Analysis of intent ought to function ministerially — as a servant — not magisterially — as lord and master — in interpreting a text; it is properly a *hermeneutic*, not a *critical* tool.

137 John Warwick Montgomery. *Human Rights & Human Dignity*. Grand Rapids, MI: Zondervan, 1986. 159-160. Professor Montgomery also addresses the issue of a "Kenotic Christ," Ibid. 160:

The suggestion that Jesus was limited to human and fallible ideas (the so-called Kenotic theory of liberal theology) also collapses under its own weight. On Kenotic reasoning, either Jesus chose to conform His statements to the fallible ideas of His time (in which case He was an opportunist who, in the spirit of Lenin, committed one of the most basic of all moral errors, that of allowing the end to justify the means); or He couldn't avoid self-limitation in the very process of incarnation (in which case incarnation is of little or no value to us, since there is then no guarantee that it reveals anything conclusive). And note that if such a dubious incarnation mixed absolute wheat with culturally relative chaff, we would have no sufficient criterion for separating them anyway, so the "absolute" portion would do us no good! To meet people's desperate need for apodictic principles of human dignity, an incarnate God must not speak with a forked tongue. In light of man's inhumanity to man, the last thing we need is additional fallible opinion, even if it is distinguished in divine dress.

has given a πλήρωμα [pleroma] of meaningfulness. May we not lose it in chasing the phantoms of analytical nonsensicality."[138]

The analytical nonsensicality of positions that attempt to hold to biblical inspiration yet reject the inerrancy of Scripture "fly directly in the face of the scriptural epistemology itself, which firmly joins 'spiritual' truth to historical, empirical facticity and regards *all* words spoken by inspiration of God as carrying their Author's guarantee of veracity."[139]

If Biblical Revelation is disqualified, *a priori*, as the authoritative source of theological truth, then what criteria could possibly be appealed to for the purpose of distinguishing truth from error *vis-à-vis* theological theorizing? Since the Scripture, by definition, could not be appealed to, then outside sources would be required. However, as already demonstrated, those same extra-biblical revelational claims are removed from the sphere of verification or falsification, and they are therefore analytically meaningless.

---

138 John Warwick Montgomery. *Crisis In Lutheran Theology*. Vol. I. 44. (Note: The bracketed "pleroma" is a trans literation of the Greek term added by the author). How can Textual Criticism re-present inerrant autographs that no longer exist? After all, if errors exist in the earliest and best manuscript copies, is it not reasonable to conclude that errors would also exist in the autographs? Professor Montgomery addresses this issue:

The answer to this latter question would certainly be yes *if* (a) the number of errors increased or even remained constant as one moved back through the textual tradition toward the time of original composition, and (b) the conservative evangelical, to solve alleged biblical errors and contradictions, hypothesized that the autographs differed materially and unjustifiably from the best copies in existence. However, (a) the number of textual errors steadily diminishes as one moves back in the direction of the lost autographs, reasonably encouraging the supposition that could we entirely fill in the interval between the originals and our earliest texts and fragments (some New Testament papyri going back to the 1st century itself), all apparent errors would disappear; and (b) the conservative evangelical only appeals to the missing autographs over against specific instances (such as the recording of numerals) where independent evidence shows a very high probability of transcriptional errors from the very outset. Whereas the believer in scriptural inerrancy will appeal (with good reason, since the phenomenon is common) to the likelihood that a very early transcriptional error produced a numerical contradiction in the extant texts, he will hardly attempt to explain alleged disharmony in the Gospel accounts of the first Easter morning by claiming that the autographs of three or the four Gospels contained no mention of the subject! In short, the conservative evangelical handles the autograph issue relative to the Bible just as a secular literary scholar handles the identical problem in reference to other ancient and many modern texts; both give the benefit of doubt to their materials, and neither should be accused of naivete' for doing so. The conservative biblical scholar goes farther, to be sure, in that he gives *maximal* benefit of doubt to his Book, but that also is justified if he has maximal reason for doing so: the clear testimony of the divine Christ that Scripture is to be trusted in all it teaches or touches ("Biblical Inerrancy: What Is At Stake?" *God's Inerrant Word*. 36-37).

139 John Warick Montgomery. *The Suicide of Christian Theology*. 284.

This point also applies to the critical issue of the self-interpreting nature of the Bible:

Were the Scripture not self-interpreting, then a "higher" revelation would be needed to provide interpretative canons for it, but such a Bible-to-the-second power cannot be shown to exist. And, indeed, there is no reason to feel that one should exist. If God inspired the Scripture, then its self-interpreting perspicuity is established. The Reformers soundly argued that the "clarity of Scripture is demanded by its inspiration. God is able to speak clearly, for He is the master of language and words."[140]

Does the Bible provide the norms, as well as the subject matter, for theological theorizing? Church history is littered with a myriad of theological norms, e.g., the primitive Greek church's emphasis on the Logos as the light shining in the darkness of man's mortality, sacramentalism in the Roman Church, justification as the normative focus of the Reformers, Protestant Modernism's emphasis on the "social gospel" and, among the more creative, Paul Tillich's concentration on Christ as the "New Being." Though theological norms have widely varied, Professor Montgomery cogently argues that normative patterns in Scripture are discoverable, as distinguished from extra-biblical norms, for theological theory formation:

In point of fact one can readily detect unsound theological norms (e.g., Modernism's "social gospel") by virtue of their inability to give biblical force to central scriptural teachings, and by their unwarranted elevation of secondary (or even unbiblical) emphases to primary position. In other words, Scripture *does* very definitely supply "weight-

---

140 Robert Preus. *The Inspiration of Scripture: A Study of the Theology of the Seventeenth Century Lutheran Dogmaticians.* Edinburgh: Oliver and Boyd. 1957. 159. Quoted in: John W. Montgomery, Ibid. 285.

ing factors" for its own teachings. Moreover, the majority of norms displayed in the history of orthodox theology have ... displayed complementary facets of the overarching biblical message that "God was in Christ, reconciling the world unto Himself." Scripture itself makes this Christo-centric teaching primary and ranges its other teachings in objective relation to it; and a sinful church learns the fact not through its historical "encounters" (which are always tainted), but from the perspicuous text of Holy Writ. Only Scripture is capable of truly interpreting Scripture; and only Scripture is able to provide the norm-structure for its interpretation and for the construction of theological doctrine based upon its inerrantly inspired content.[141]

Concluding Professor Montgomery's discussion of the scientific level of theological theorizing, we must reaffirm that the scientific theorizer and the theologian formulate and test their respective theories in much the same manner. The scientific theorizer attempts to relate to Nature intelligibly *vis-à-vis* the formulation of conceptual Gestalts (hypotheses, theories, laws) and, as well, the theologian attempts the coherent *fitting of the facts* and reflection of the norms of Holy Scripture through the employment of conceptual Gestalts (doctrines, dogmas). A comparison of scientific and theological theorizing is as follows:[142]

---

141 Ibid. 287.
142 Ibid. 288.

	SCIENCE	THEOLOGY
THE DATA (Epistemological Certainty presupposed)	NATURE	THE BIBLE
CONCEPTUAL GESTALTS (In order of decreasing certainty)	LAWS	Ecumenical Creeds (e.g., the Apostles' Creed) and historic Confessions: e.g., the Augsburg Confession)
	THEORIES	Theological systems (e.g. Calvin's *Institutes*)
	HYPOTHESES	Theological proposals (e.g. Gustaf Aulen's *Christus Victor*)

Regarding the table above, Montgomery specifically references Conceptual Gestalts, "In order of decreasing certainty," in the following explanation:

'Absolute' certainty, both in science and in theology, rests only with the data (for the former, natural phenomena; for the latter, scriptural affirmations). All conceptualizations on the basis of these data lack ultimate certainty (in science the Einsteinian revolution helped to make this clear), but some formulations are so well attested by the data that they acquire a practically (though not a theoretically) "certain" status; in science we call such Gestalts "laws," in theology, "creeds" and "confessions." Just as a denial of scientific laws removes one from the scientific community (cf. modern alchemists such as Tiffereau and Jullivet-Castelot), so denial of creeds and confessions results in one's separation from ecclesiastical circles. Scientific hypotheses

61

and theological proposals, however, are never proper tests of "fellowship," for they lie, by definition, in the realm of open questions — which, hopefully, more investigation will either raise to a higher status or cause to be discarded. Scientific "theories" (in the narrow sense) and theological systems occupy an intermediate position between laws/creeds — confessions and hypotheses/theological proposals, thus, although they are not generally made the basis of 'formal' tests of fellowship, they often have that function on an informal (social or psychological) level.[143]

THE ARTISTIC AND SACRAL LEVELS OF THEOLOGIAL THEORY FORMATION[144]

Beyond the objective, scientific level of theological formation, the theorizer is required to pass into the subjective, experiential realms of the *artistic* and the *sacral* where "the ability to perceive

---

143 Ibid. 308, footnote #71.

144 Professor Montgomery's theological methodology mirrors Luther's. (Luther's theological methodology is defined and explained in footnote #89 above. The repeating of the Reformer's methodology here is for the convenience of the reader). The Reformer drew his methodology from Scripture:

Let me show you a right method for studying theology, the one that I have used. If you adopt it, you will become so learned that if it were necessary, you yourself would be qualified to produce books just as good as those of the Fathers and the church councils. Even as I dare to be so bold in God as to pride myself, without arrogance or lying, as not being greatly behind some of the Fathers in the matter of making books; as to my life, I am far from being their equal. This method is the one which the pious king David teaches in the 119th Psalm and which, no doubt, was practiced by all the Patriarchs and Prophets. In the 119th Psalm you will find three rules which are abundantly expounded throughout the entire Psalm. They are called: *Oratio, Meditatio, Tentatio.*

Meditatio, in Luther's thought, is a reference to the reading, study and meditation of the Holy Scripture. The level of *Tentatio* refers to subjective, experiential involvement and the *Oratio* is the level of prayer, intimate contact with the Holy One, without which all theologizing is futile.

Classical Protestant orthodoxy's understanding of faith also displays this threefold approach to theology: the concept of faith is initiated at the level of *Notitia* ("knowledge" — referring to the objective, scientific element), *Assensus* ("assent" – subjective, experiential involvement), and *Fiducia* ("trust/confidence" – the vertical regenerating relation with God in Christ).

inner meaning" is demanded.[145] Professor Montgomery's empirical methodology combines faith and belief, following from the retroductive inference of causal influences in space-time, ordinary history, as two aspects of one act.[146] Therefore, Montgomery insists that "Theorizing in the humanities or social sciences requires more than scientific objectivity; it also demands 'the language of experience'[147] – grasping the *point* or *meaning* of what is being done or said."[148]

Departing from the external, objective level of the scientific, we must now "make the equally important point that, by virtue of its historical character, the biblical revelation lies also in the realm of the social sciences and humanities. Because God revealed Himself in history and the Bible – the source of all true theological Gestalts – is a historical document, theological theories must partake of the dual science-art character of historical methodology."[149] Reformed theologian, J.I. Packer observes that at the artistic level of theological theorizing, "one tries to live by the truth one knows" and this is what makes the theologian, for "Theological insight must be sought *in via* not in an armchair."[150]

---

145   Ibid. 288. John Montgomery is the editor of *Christianity for the Toughminded* wherein James R. Moore, "Science and Christianity," page 88, rhetorically addresses the significance of the artistic and sacral levels involved in theological theorizing:

The application of scientific method to history has these features. But it also has at least one drawback: experimentation 'qua' science in efforts to establish and experience personally the identity of a historical figure is impossible. If we had lived in Jesus' day we might have "experimented" by becoming his personal friends – perhaps even his disciples. In a personal relationship with him his true character would be revealed far more clearly than by the data of any historical narrative. But what about today? Is it possible to conclude our scientific search for God by actually making his acquaintance?

146   John Warwick Montgomery. *Where Is History Going?* 164.

147   John Ciardi. "How Does a Poem Mean?" In *An Introduction to Literature*, ed. Gordon N. Ray. Boston, MA: Houghton Mifflin. 1959. 666. In John Warwick Montgomery. *The Suicide of Christian Theology*. 290.

148   Peter Winch. *The Idea of a Social Science and Its Relation to Philosophy*. London: Routledge & Kegan Paul. 1958. 115. In John Warwick Montgomery. Ibid.

149   John Warwick Montgomery. *The Suicide of Christian Theology*. 290.

150   J.I. Packer. Systematic Theology I notes, (18), "Christian Theological Methodology," Regent College, Vancouver, B.C., Canada, Spring, 1989.

Luther's contentions, concerning the Fall of man, penetrate to the point concerning "the language of experience" at the artistic level of theological theorizing: "You should read the story of

THE SACRAL LEVEL OF THEOLOGICAL THEORIZING

In common with science, theological theorizing begins at the objective level of empirical observation; the next level of theological theorizing, the artistic, engages the theologian with the "inner meaning" of his subject — God's revelation in the Bible — much like the social scientist. However, beyond science or the humanities, theology engages a dimension unique to itself — the sacral or holy. Montgomery contends that "Lack of recognition of the distance between sinful man and sinless God or blindness to the absolute necessity of relying upon His Holy Spirit in theologizing will vitiate efforts in this realm, even though the scientific and artistic requirements are fully met. Without 'Fiducia,' 'Notitia,' and 'Assensus' are like sounding brass and tinkling cymbal."[151]

The "Sacral" is conveyed in theological theory formation by means of humble acknowledgment of God's "otherness":

> Ian Ramsey, ...observes the linguistically "odd" character of genuine theological affirmations. These consist of models taken from experience, so qualified to indicate their sacral (logically "odd") character. Such "qualified models" can be found throughout the range of Christian doctrine, e.g., in the phrases "first cause," "infinite wisdom," "eternal purpose" (where the qualifying adjective in each case points the empirically grounded noun in the direction of the sacral, so as to reduce anthropomorphism and increase awareness of God's "otherness."[152]

The "odd" qualifier, pointed to by Ramsey, directs us back to the Bible as the sole, normative source of theological theorizing:

---

the Fall as if it happened yesterday, and to you" — See John Warwick Montgomery's article, "The Cause and Cure of Sin," *Resource*, III. February 1962. 2-4.

151 John Warwick Montgomery. *The Suicide of Christian Theology*. 292.

152 Ibid. 293.

Only the Bible can serve as an adequate guide for determining what sacral qualifiers are "suitable" to given doctrinal formulations.... Sacred Scripture offers the sole criterion for testing the scientific, the artistic, and the sacral health of theological theories. Does a given theory represent objective truth? Does it incorporate the proper kind of subjective involvement? Does it adequately preserve the sacred dimension? To all three of these questions *Sola Scriptura* holds the answers.[153]

How does synthesis of the scientific, artistic, and the holy take place? Great care must be taken here, for reductionism *vis-à-vis* theological theorizing, occurs often because of negligence concerning the synthetic problem.

The biblical evidence moves us to conclude that each of the three levels involved in theological theorizing, e.g., the scientific, artistic, and sacral, are *absolutely* essential to the task of the theologian:

Neither the scientific, nor the artistic, nor the sacral element can be removed from theological theorizing without destroying the possibility of results in harmony with God's Word. Thus, we can legitimately expect to find deleterious theological climates wherever in church history or in the present reductionism is permitted with reference to one or more of the three methodological elements.[154]

Christian history, in every age, is marked by theological reductionisms which continually threaten to "shipwreck" the faith of the church. The table below demonstrates combinations of methodological reductionisms:[155]

---

153 Ibid. 294.

154 Ibid. 295.

155 Ibid. Note: Entry five (5) in the table identifies a resulting reductionism as a "Theology of Glory." Dr. Montgomery comments that, "Luther used the expression 'Theologia crucis' ('Theology

REDUCTION OF	INTO	PRODUCES
1. Artistic & Sacral	Scientific	Dead Orthodoxy
2. Scientific & Sacral	Artistic	Pietism
3. Scientific & Artistic	Sacral	Mysticism
4. Sacral	Scientific & Artistic	Anthropocentrism
5. Artistic	Scientific & Sacral	"Theology of Glory"
6. Scientific	Artistic & Sacral	Existentialism

Montgomery observes that twentieth century theologizing was "... particularly prone to reductionism' — (6), which eliminates the scientific layer from theology, and produces wooly-minded, unverifiable existentialisms that readily pass into the realm of analytic meaninglessness."[156]

How should the three levels involved in theological theorizing be related for the purpose of avoiding theological reductionisms? Professor Montgomery stresses that, "we must structure the scientific, the artistic, and the sacral factors in theology so that they have a theocentric, Cross-centered focus, and so that the objective provides an epistemological check on the artistic; and the artistic serves as an entrée to the sacral."[157]

The scientific, artistic, and sacral levels, involved in theological theorizing, must revolve around the objective, historical event of the Cross for the purpose of avoiding reductionisms. The follow-

---

of the Cross'); see Philip S. Watson. *Let God Be God! An Interpretation of the Theology of Martin Luther.* London: Epworth Press. 1947. 78. The scholastics erred through neglecting the 'Tentatio' element requisite to the theologian's activity: their impossible endeavor to theologize from as it were, the perspective of God's throne would not have come about if they had retained awareness of their own subjective involvement in the theological task." Ibid. 310-311.

156 Ibid. 295.

157 Ibid. 296.

ing structural model represents the substantive-conceptual reality of Professor Montgomery's empirical theological methodology:

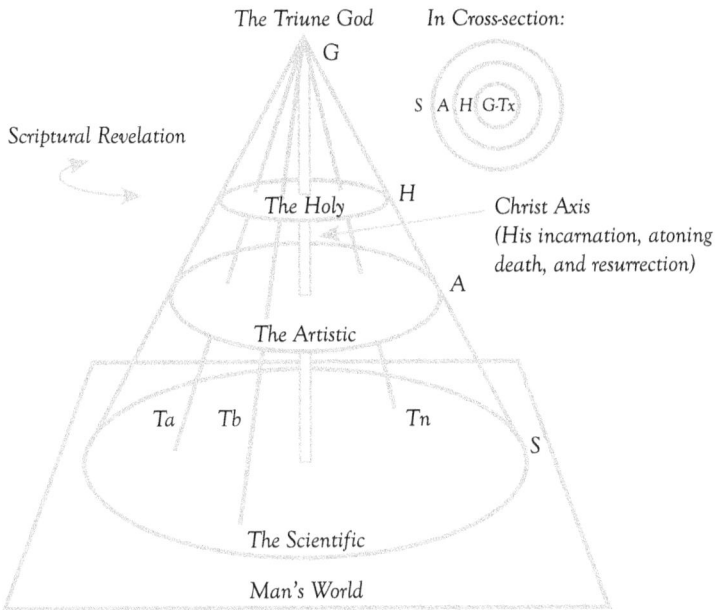

The Triune God
G

In Cross-section:

S A H G-Tx

Scriptural Revelation

The Holy H

Christ Axis
(His incarnation, atoning death, and resurrection)

A

The Artistic

Ta   Tb   Tn

S

The Scientific

Man's World

JOHN WARWICK MONTGOMERY'S THEOLOGICAL MODEL

Fredrick Ferre' ("Mapping the Logic of Models in Science and Theology") defines "model" in terms of the *type, scope and status*. Professor Montgomery refers to the aforementioned article by Ferre' in his "The Theologian's Craft: A Discussion of Theory Formation and Theory Testing in Theology."[158]

A model's *type* refers to its "concreteness," that is, is it necessary to build an actual model or may it be pictured or perhaps merely conceived? The *scope* of a model involves the inclusiveness

---

158   Fredrick Ferre. "Mapping the Logic of Models in Science and Theology." *The Christian Scholar*. XLVI. Spring 1963, is criticized by Dr. Montgomery: "I am not happy with certain interpretations in this article, e.g., the author's distinction between theories and models; his belief that scientific theories, unlike theological theories, can exist without models), but in general the article deserves the highest commendation for its incisive wrestling with an exceedingly important methodological issue" — "The Theologian's Craft." *The Suicide of Christian Theology*. 301.

of the model — how much reality is the model supposed to represent? Finally, the *status* of a model involves its indispensableness (i.e., is the model necessary or even helpful rather than potentially dangerous?).[159] Judgments concerning the model's status may vary regarding the different attributions of type and scope.

Ferre' defines model as "that which provides epistemological vividness or immediacy to a theory by offering as an interpretation of the abstract or unfamiliar theory-structure something that both fits the logical form of the theory and is well known."[160] For a logical analysis of a theory to take place, the representative model must allow for the distinguishing of those elements that are "relevant" and those that are "irrelevant." The theological model, however, is not meant to provide epistemological immediacy of the abstract concept, "God." One of the tasks, therefore, of the theologian is to distinguish between what may be taken as "logically relevant" and what may be considered "logically irrelevant" features of the Deity as disclosed in Revelation.

The challenge that confronts the theologian involves the rigorous interpretation of the key epistemological assertions of holy scripture — "He who has seen me has seen the Father; how can you say, 'show me the Father'?"[161] Ferre' asserts, "Every Christological formulation that takes that statement seriously is, whether consciously or not, a study in epistemology and an exercise in model-reading."[162]

---

159 Frederick Ferre'. "Mapping the Logic of Models in Science and Theology." 9-39. In explanation of what he means by "dangerous," Ferre' remarks:

We are warned, by those who consider the status of the model to be primarily dangerous incitement to metaphorical thinking, against approaching the use of a model literally, expecting the wrong things from it; we are also well warned, by those who look at models as primarily convenient luxuries, against adopting models uncritically being lured off into pseudo questions by logical irrelevancies. However, in defense of the use of models, Ferre' asserts: But we are now prepared to proceed, vigilantly but aware that models can add great power to our cognitive pursuits, with the knowledge that, risky or not, models put a tool in our hand for understanding what, without models, may remain opaque. Ibid. 23.

160 Ibid. 24.

161 John 14:9 (RSV).

162 Fredrick Ferre', "Mapping the Logic of Models in Science and Theology." 26. s

Ferre' concludes in stating that epistemological vividness, *vis-à-vis* theological models, can be demonstrated through the application of five tests: (1) Do the propositions that purport to attribute structure to the model follow *consistently*, i.e., without contradiction? (2) Is *coherence* or external consistency demonstrated in a universal manner, i.e. are all bodies of knowledge integrated by the model? (3) Is the model *applicable* to individual experience? (4) Does the model *adequately* apply to all domains of feeling and perception? (5) Is the model *effective* as an instrument in coping with the total environment of human experience?[163]

The application of Ferre's five tests, for the purpose of evaluating the epistemological vividness of Professor Montgomery's Theological Model, commence with five heuristic propositions that attribute structure; and culminate in proposition 6, a definitive description of the universal scope of Montgomery's philosophy of history:

1. On the basis of accepted principles of textual and historical analysis, the Gospel records are found to be trustworthy historical documents — primary source evidence for the life of Christ.

2. In these records, Jesus exercises divine prerogatives and claims to be God in human flesh; and He rests His claims on His forthcoming resurrection.

3. In all four Gospels, Christ's bodily resurrection is described in minute detail; Christ's resurrection evidences His deity.

4. The fact of the resurrection cannot be discounted on *a priori*, philosophical grounds; miracles are impossible only if one so defines them — but such definition rules out proper historical investigation.

---

163 Kent Bendall and Frederick Ferre'. *Exploring the Logic of Faith.* New York: Association Press, 1962. 166f.

5. If Christ is God, then He speaks the truth concerning the absolute divine authority of the Old Testament and of the soon-to-be-written New Testament; concerning His death for the sins of the world; and concerning the nature of man and of history.

6. It follows from the preceding that all Biblical assertions bearing on philosophy of history is to be regarded as revealed truth, and that all human attempts at historical interpretation are to be judged for truth-value on the basis of harmony with Scriptural revelation.[164]

God's propositional revelation to man is represented by the cone. God's historical self disclosure to man begins at the detached scientific level of irreducible facts. The theologian constructs his cellophane tubes from bottom to top, skillfully gathering and presenting revelational truth. The myriad of truths, e.g., Ta, Tb, Tn, etc., revealed in holy Scripture, all revolve around the "Christ-Axis," the centralized truth of God's revelation — the Incarnation of the Word, the Cross and the Resurrection.[165]

Following his exegesis of Scripture, the theologian relates Biblical truths to both the axis — e.g., the Incarnate Christ, the Cross, the Resurrection, and the Triune God — and to each other (the truths of revelation are represented by the distances separating Ta, Tb and Tx). The theologian will transmit his data into intelligible patterns (Gestalts) endeavoring to formulate doctrinal constructions that "'fit' the revelational truths in their mutual relations."[166] The model's "theological theories can be conceived of as cellophane tubes constructed to fit with maximum transparency the truths of revelation; the theologian will endeavor continu-

---

164   John Warwick Montgomery. *The Shape of the Past.* 138-39.

165   Montgomery. *Where Is History Going?* 160.

166   Montgomery. *The Suicide of Christian Theology.* 297.

ally to 'tighten' them so that they will most accurately capture the essence of biblical truth."[167]

The upward assent of faith involves the subjective commitment of the theologian at the artistic level — The artistic element of theological theorizing brings the theologian into personal involvement with his Subject's (The holy Trinity's) "inner meaning." Professor Montgomery affirms that both Christian epistemology and experience are preserved in the substantive conceptual reality of sacred Scripture — The objective (the scientific) provides an epistemological check to the artistic; and the artistic serves to access the sacral, the realm of grace and judgment.[168]

Montgomery continues to explain the artistic and sacral levels of theological theorizing:

> The application of scientific method to history has ... at least one drawback: experimentation 'qua' science in efforts to establish and experience personally the identity of a historical figure is impossible. If we had lived in Jesus' day we might have "experimented" by becoming his personal friends — perhaps even his disciples. In a personal relationship with him his true character would be revealed far more clearly than by the data of any historical narrative. But what about today? Is it possible to conclude our scientific search for God by actually making his acquaintance?[169]

The theory construction of the worthy theologian brings him to the level of the sacred where both the impersonal "it" of the scientific and the subjective "I" of the artistic bow in humble ado-

---

167   Ibid. 297.

168   Ibid. 296

169   *Christianity for the Tough Minded.* Edited by John Warwick Montgomery. Minneapolis, MN. Bethany House Publishers, 1973. 88.

ration of the Divine[170] – "*Christianity provides the only verifiable assurance that life has eternal purpose.*"[171] Making "his acquaintance" leads to final confirmation and "assures us of ultimate fulfillment."[172]

John Warwick Montgomery's Christo-centric theological model represents a total synthesis of reality – *The "epistemological vividness" of Montgomery's model provides theologians with an interpretative net.*[173] Part 3 – Verification of Montgomery's empirical theological methodology establishes his Theological Model as representative of substantive-conceptual reality.

---

170 Montgomery. *The Suicide of Christian Theology.* 297. Professor Montgomery illustrates the doctrinal formulation of the Trinity, *vis-à-vis* his theological model. Ibid. 297-99.

171 Ibid. 202.

172 Montgomery. *Tractatus Logico-Theologicus.* 203.

173 Montgomery. *The Suicide of Christian Theology.* 272-73.

PART 3:

VERIFYING MONTGOMERY'S LEGAL-HISTORICAL METHODOLOGY

CHAPTER THREE

THE TRUSTWORTHINESS OF THE NEW TESTAMENT

"As I have tried to show in my Shape of the Past,
the meaning of history (which is, after all, a special case of
the meaning of life) can be discovered only if man has in fact
received an objectively reliable Revelation originating from
outside the blooming, buzzing, confused human situation"

— John Warwick Montgomery.[174]

The scope of Dr. Montgomery's Theological Model is stated in proposition six of his outline of a Christian worldview: "It follows from the preceding [propositions 1-5] that all Biblical assertions bearing on philosophy of history is to be regarded as revealed truth, and that all human attempts at historical interpretation are to be judged for truth-value on the basis of harmony with Scrip-

---

174   John Warwick Montgomery. *Where Is History Going?* Appendix E. 240-41.

tural revelation"[175] — "The plain consequence is that the only possible answer to modern man's quest for the meaning of history and for an absolute ethical standard would have to lie in a revelation from outside the world."[176]

THE VERACITY OF THE NEW TESTAMENT DOCUMENTS

"The New Testament documents are the primary-source records for the determination of Jesus' life and work and are historically veracious"

— John Warwick Montgomery.[177]

We do not possess the autographs, i.e., the original New Testament documents. We therefore must reconstruct the New Testament from existing manuscript tradition. The reconstruction of the text of the New Testament will be accomplished using the same literary tests employed by secular scholars to determine the trustworthiness of ancient documents: the bibliographical, the internal and the external tests.[178]

THE BIBLIOGRAPHICAL TEST

The bibliographical test is primarily concerned with the reconstruction of an ancient document, in this case, the autographs of the New Testament. The lower textual critic's reconstruction of the New Testament focuses on: (1) how the text, in this case the New Testament, has reached us; (2) the number of available

---

175   Montgomery. *The Shape of the Past*. 138.

176   Montgomery. *The Suicide of Christian Theology*. 366.

177   Montgomery. *Tractatus Logio-Theologicus*. 74.

178   C. Sanders. *Introduction to Research in English Literary History*. New York: Macmillan. 1952, 143ff.

manuscripts and fragments, and (3) the time interval separating the autographs (the originals) and the oldest extant fragments or manuscripts (copies of the autographs).[179]

Sir Frederick G. Kenyon, formerly the director and principal librarian of the British Museum, testifies to the superiority of the New Testament manuscript evidence over other ancient manuscript evidence:

> In no other case is the interval of time between the composition of the book and the date of the earliest extant manuscripts so short as in that of the New Testament. The books of the New Testament were written in the latter part of the first century; the earliest extant manuscripts (trifling scraps excepted) are of the fourth century — say, from 250-300 years later. This may sound a considerable interval, but it is nothing to that which parts most of the great classical authors from their earliest manuscripts. We believe that we have in all essentials an accurate text of the seven extant plays of Sophocles; yet the earliest substantial manuscript upon which it is based was written more than 1400 years after the poet's death. Aeschylus, Aristophanes, and Thucydides are in the same state; while with Euripides the interval increased to 1600 years. For Plato it may be put at 1300 years, for Demosthenes as low as 1200.[180]

Following Kenyon's original bibliographical attestation to the New Testament, several papyri were discovered that dated back to the end of the first century, bringing the time interval between

---

179 For a thorough study of the bibliographical test involving New Testament tradition, see, Bruce Metzger. *A Textual Commentary on the Greek New Testament.* Stuttgart, Germany. United Bible Society. 1971. Introduction — Metzger presents a clear, detailed development of (1) the history of the transmission of the New Testament; (2) the primary criteria used in choosing among conflicting witnesses to the text and (3) the principal witnesses to the New Testament listed according to text types.

180 Sir Fredrick G. Kenyon. *Handbook to the Textual Criticism of the New Testament.* 2nd ed. London: Macmillan. 1912. 5. In Montgomery. *History and Christianity.* Minneapolis, MN.: Bethany Fellowship. 1970. 27.

the actual composition of the New Testament and the fragments to within but a few years.[181] These discoveries prompted Kenyon to write: "The interval, then, between the dates of original composition and the earliest extant evidence becomes so small as to be in fact negligible, and the last foundation for any doubt that the Scriptures have come down to us substantially as they were written has now been removed. Both the authenticity and the general integrity of the books of the New Testament may be regarded as finally established."[182]

Montgomery further asserts: "Moreover, as A.T. Robertson, the author of the most comprehensive grammar of New Testament Greek, wrote, 'There are some 8,000 manuscripts of the Latin Vulgate and at least 1,000 for the other early versions. Add over 4,000 Greek manuscripts[183] and we have 13,000 manuscript copies of portions of the New Testament. Besides all this, much of the New Testament can be reproduced from the quotations of the early Christian writers.'"[184] The rich textual tradition of the New Testament has yielded an abundance of manuscript evidence for the reconstruction of the autographs — by comparison

---

181   See F.W. Hall. MS. *Authorities for the Text of the Chief Classical Writers. Companion to Classical Texts.* Oxford: Clarendon Press, 1913. 199ff. (Hall's comparison of ancient texts follows in this chapter).

182   Sir Fredick G. Kenyon. The Bible and Archaeology. New York: Harper, 1940. 288-89. In Montgomery. Ibid. 28.

183   Dr. Sean McDowell, "What is the Most Recent Manuscript Count for the New Testament?", estimates that **5,856** Greek (*Κοινή*) Manuscripts are now the significant part of New Testament Textual Tradition. https://seanmcdowell.org/blog/what-is-the-most-recent-manuscript-count-for-the-new-testament.

 Professor Sean McDowell comments that, "Scholars use different sources, such as the Leuven Database (https://www.trismegistos.org/ldab/) or the Center for the Study of New Testament Manuscripts (It is extremely laborious to track down the number of both classical and biblical manuscripts. We had a team of researchers and scholars help us with this endeavor." See also: Josh McDowell & Sean McDowell, *Evidence That Demands a Verdict: Life Changing Truth for a Skeptical World.* Thomas Nelson, 2017 (Updated: Josh McDowell. *Evidence The Demands A Verdict.* Volume I, April 1990).

184   A.T. Robertson. *Introduction to the Textual Criticism of the New Testament.* Nashville, TN.: Broadman Press, 1925. 70. John Warwick Montgomery. Ibid. 28-29.

 Princeton's Bruce Metzger computes a total of 4,969 New Testament Greek MSS. *The Text of the New Testament.* New York: Oxford University Press. 1964. 31-33. More recently, Kurt and Barbara Aland account for 5,487 Greek MSS. *The Text of The New Testament.* Grand Rapids, MI.: Wm. B. Eerdmans, 1989. 74.

to other ancient texts, the available number of New Testament manuscripts and fragments is staggering![185]

Moreover, the late Biblical archaeologist William F. Albright, Johns Hopkins University, confidently concluded: "In my opinion, every book of the New Testament was written by a baptized Jew between the forties and the eighties of the first century A.D. (very probably sometime between about A.D. 50 and 75)."[186] And thus, the time interval between the autographs and the earliest extant manuscripts not only firmly places the writing of the New Testament in the first century, it is, as well, much too brief for layers of legends and myths to form around the testimony of the Christian Scriptures. The significance of our discussion is illustrated in F.W. Hall's chart comparing numerous other ancient texts with the New Testament:[187]

AUTHOR	DATE WRITTEN	EARLIEST COPY	TIME SPAN	COPIES
Caesar	100–44 B.C.	900 A.D.	1000 Years	10
Plato: (Tetralogies)	427–347 B.C.	900 A.D.	1200 Years	7
Tacitus: (Annals) and Minor Works	100 A.D.	1100 A.D.	1000 Years	10 (–)
Pliny the Younger (History)	61–113 A.D.	850 A.D.	750 Years	7

185   The John Rylands fragment contains 5 verses from John 18; it is (liberally) dated from about 125 A.D. The significance of this "trifling scrap" cannot be underestimated; John is the last surviving apostle, and his writing closes out the New Testament. This being the case, the entire canon of the New Testament is placed firmly in the first century.

186   William F. Albright. Interview: *Christianity Today.* 18 January 1963.

187   F.W. Hall. "Manuscript Authorities for the Text of the Chief Classical Writers." *A Companion to Classical Texts.* Oxford: Clarendon Press, 1913. And Bruce Metzger. *The History of New Testament Textual Criticism.* Grand Rapids, MI.: Wm. B. Eerdmans, 1963.

Thucydides: (History)	460–400 B.C.	900 A.D.	1300 Years	8
Heroditus: (History)	480–425 B.C.	900 A.D.	1300 Years	8
Sophocles	496–406 B.C.	1000 A.D.	1400 Years	193
Aristotle	384–322 B.C.	1100 A.D.	1400 Years	49(+)
Demosthenes	383–322 B.C.	1100 A.D.	1300 Years	200
Homer	900 B.C.	400 B.C.	500 Years	643
New Testament	48–110 A.D.	125 A.D.	15–90 Years	20,000 (+)

The reader will observe, for example, that concerning all but two of the classics listed above (excluding the New Testament), a millennium or more separates the autographs (the original documents) from the earliest extant manuscripts. And further, the reader will note the relative limited number of available manuscripts used by the textual critic for the reconstruction of the particular classic's autographs. Comparatively, the bibliographical evidence for the Scriptures is so substantial that to "be skeptical of the resultant text of the New Testament books is to allow all of classical antiquity to slip into obscurity, for no documents of the ancient period are as well attested bibliographically as the New Testament."[188]

---

188 John Warwick Montgomery. *History and Christianity.* 29. The whole of the New Testament canon requires dating before 70 A.D. Why? Jerusalem was leveled (to include the Temple) by the Roman military in 70 A.D. and this event is not mentioned by any of the New Testament writers. Additionally, we know the Apostle Paul died during Nero's reign. Nero's brutal persecution of the Christians was in A.D. 64. Since the Apostle was still alive at the close of Acts, Acts had to have been written before A.D. 64. Luke and Acts were originally one document; Acts is the continuation of Luke and therefore, Luke predates Acts. And Mark was written before Luke, as even liberal scholarship acknowledges. Mark's Gospel was then written in the 50's only twenty years removed from the events of Christ's crucifixion and resurrection. Paul authored Romans in the mid 50's, most probably A.D. 54. In the opening lines of his letter to the Romans, Paul proclaims the Lordship of Jesus Christ through his resurrection from the dead. And Galatians, which was also authored by Paul in the mid-50's, records Paul's meeting with the Apostle Peter, one of Jesus' first disciples and James, the Lord's younger brother, some fourteen years earlier.

THE INTERNAL TEST

In this second test, historical and literary analysis follows Aristotle's dictum — the benefit of the doubt is given to the document.[189] Therefore, the critic must "listen to the claims of the document under analysis and not assume fraud or error unless the author disqualifies himself by contradictions or known factual inaccuracies."[190]

The truth claims of the New Testament include descriptions of miracles. But doubt is to be given to the document, not arrogated by the critic to himself — no historian or literary critic can dismiss documentary evidence on the *a priori* grounds that its record of remarkable events may be in conflict with their particular worldview. To the contrary, "if the documents are sufficiently reliable, the remarkable events must be accepted even if they cannot be successfully explained by analogy with other events or by an *a priori* scheme of natural causation."[191]

The Apostle John contended, in common with the other eyewitnesses to the life of Christ, (e.g., Lk. 1:1-4, Acts 2:32, 2 Pt. 1:16): "The man who saw it has given testimony, and his testimony is true. He knows that he tells the truth, and he testifies so that you also may believe" (John 19:35). The value of eyewitness testimony, such as John's, is addressed by Lutheran theologian, Rod Rosenbladt:

The New Testament, particularly Paul's epistles (all of which predate the Gospels) unveils a divine picture of Jesus. The theology of the New Testament portrait of Jesus of Nazareth is that he is God incarnate; the New Testament's high Christology is developed within a mere ten to twenty years after the crucifixion.

189 Roman law asserts: "... when the witnesses for the parties gave conflicting testimony on any point, it was the duty of the judge, not to count the number on each side, but to consider which of them were entitled to the greatest credit, according to the well-known rule, 'Testimonia ponderanda sunt, no numerando.' ... The Roman law provided that the benefit of the doubt should be given to the defendant rather than to the plaintiff" (Lord Mackenzie, *Studies in Roman Law, with Comparative Views of the Laws of France, England, and Scotland;* cf. J. Wybo, *De interrogationibus in jure* [1732]). In: John Warwick Montgomery. *Tractatus Logico-Theologicus.* 3.12513. 71.

190 Ibid.

191 Ibid. 21.

81

The survival of the Christian faith in the midst of so hostile an atmosphere shows full well that its appeal to well known facts was irrefutable. Instead of transferring Christianity into the realm of transcendent, unverifiable "truths," the writers multiplied chances of criticism by stressing detail upon detail. No opportunity for cross-examination was bypassed, yet the enemies of the Gospel (including both Roman and Jewish authorities) were not able to produce evidence which would have effectively countered the claims of the apostles and evangelists.[192]

Not only was Christianity's ability to survive in the hostile environment of first century Palestine a testimony to the factual accuracy of the disciples' claims, the disciples themselves invited scrutiny of their claims! Peter's sermon during the Feast of Pentecost boldly challenged his massive audience to examine the evidentiary claims for the Resurrection themselves — "*as you yourselves know*" (cf. Acts 2:22-24).

Paul's preaching was typical of apostolic preaching, and therefore, it did not depart from Peter's bold challenges. For example, in his trial before King Agrippa and Festus (Acts 26), the Apostle did not transfer the claims of the Gospel to "the realm of transcendent, unverifiable 'truths'" but instead claimed that the atoning death and resurrection of Jesus Christ were actual historical events and further, these events were in fulfillment of Moses and the prophets (King Agrippa was familiar with the Jewish customs and controversies and, he was well acquainted with the prophets).

However, the skeptic Festus interrupted Paul's testimony saying, "You are out of your mind, Paul!" But Paul continued, strengthening his defense by contending: "What I am saying is true and reasonable. The king is familiar with these things, and

---

192 Rod Rosenbladt. "The Integrity of the Gospel Writers." *Christianity For The Tough Minded*. Edited by: John W. Montgomery. Minneapolis, MN: Bethany House Publishers. 1973. 240.

I can speak freely to him. I am convinced that none of this has escaped his notice, because it was not done *in a corner*" — Paul's testimony was *public*; the historical evidence supporting the Apostle's proclamation of the Gospel was open to the investigation of the unbelieving authorities before whom he was testifying.

But what about alleged discrepancies in the Gospel accounts of Christ's resurrection? There exist enough differences among the writers of the New Testament so as to discount any allegations of conspiracy. Yet, at the same time, such substantial agreement exists among the inspired authors so as to demonstrate that they in fact were all well acquainted with the same great historical event. Simon Greenleaf contends that the "discrepancies between the narratives of the several evangelists, when carefully examined, will not be found sufficient to invalidate their testimony. Many seeming contradictions will prove, upon closer scrutiny, to be in substantial agreement; and it may be confidently asserted that there are none that will not yield, under fair and just criticism."[193] The author's accounts provide us with a built-in means to cross-examine each of them — this is non-existent outside of the Christian faith.

THE EXTERNAL TEST

The external test inquires: "Do other historical materials confirm or deny the internal testimony provided by the documents themselves?"[194] External testimony from historians, satirists, politicians, and playwrights from the first and second centuries consistently confirms the testimony of the writers of the New Testament.

Among the multiple sources of historical corroborations of the New Testament is the Roman historian, Cornelius Tacitus

---

193   Simon Greenleaf. *Testimony of the Evangelists.* Grand Rapids, MI: Baker Book House. 1984. 33. See also, Gleason Archer Jr. *Encyclopedia of Bible Difficulties.* Minneapolis, MN: Bethany House. 1982. This work is an exhaustive, scholarly treatment of alleged contradictions in the Bible.

194   John Warwick Montgomery. *History and Christianity.* 31.

(AD 112) who writes of the death of Jesus Christ and the influence of Christians in Rome. Tacitus states that Pontius Pilate put Jesus to death during the reign of Tiberius (*Annals* XV.44). Tacitus further mentions the burning of the temple in Jerusalem in A.D. 70 and he refers to Christianity in that context (*Histories*, Chron. ii. 30.6).

Lucian of Samosta, a second century satirist, ridiculed Christianity. Lucian spoke of the rejection of polytheism by Christians and stated that the primitive Christian Church worshipped Jesus "like a god." He also refers to the crucifixion of Jesus Christ in Palestine (*The Passing of Peregrinus*).

The first century Jewish historian, Flavius Josephus (AD 37-100) mentions Jesus Christ and his relationship to the primitive Church stating that the first Christians believed their Lord had risen from the dead following his crucifixion under Pontius Pilate. Josephus further speaks of Christ's miracles (*Antiquities*, 28:33). Regarding Josephus, F.F. Bruce further informs us:

> Here, in the pages of Josephus, we meet many figures who are well known to us from the New Testament: the colourful family of the Herods; the Roman emperors Augustus, Tiberius, Claudius, and Nero; Quirinius, the governor of Syria; Pilate, Felix, and Festus, the procurators of Judea; the high priestly families — Annas, Caiaphas, Ananias, and the rest; the Pharisees and the Sadducees; and so on.[195]

Another Roman historian, Suetonius (c. AD 120), refers to the persecution of Christians by Nero (*Life of the Caesars*, 26:2). In a letter dated AD 73, a Syrian named Mara Bar-Serapian mentions the death of Jesus Christ in addition to the deaths of Socrates and Pythagoras. This letter is presently preserved at the British Museum.

---

195 F.F. Bruce. *The New Testament Documents, Are They Reliable?* Downers Grove, ILL.: InterVarsity Press. 1977. 104.

A Samaritan historian, Thallus (c. AD 52) records the darkness that covered the earth during the crucifixion of Jesus of Nazareth. Thallus sought a naturalistic explanation for the darkness, such as a solar eclipse as mentioned by Julius Africanus (the third book of *Histories*). Julius Africanus argued against Thallus' theory for the darkness present on the day of Christ's crucifixion. Philegon, a first-century historian, also mentions the darkness on the day of Christ's death (*Histories*, cited by Julius Africanus).[196]

Pliny the Younger (c. AD 112) noted in a letter that Christians worshipped Jesus Christ as a god and that they came together once a week to sing hymns to their Savior. He mentions his own persecution of Christians and his having killed many of them while governor of Bithynia. He stated that he tried to force Christians to "curse Christ, which a genuine Christian cannot be induced to do" (*Epistles* X.96).

The Jewish Talmud refers to the ministry of Jesus of Nazareth, attributes his miracles to demonic origins, asserts he was born out of adultery; and refers to his crucifixion on the eve of the Passover (*Sanhedrin* 43a, "Eve of Passover," and *Yebamoth* 4, 3; 49a).[197]

Francis Beckwith's summary findings of the external, non-Christian references sufficiently substantiate the internal claims of the Gospel as to its central doctrines:

(1) Jesus was worshipped and believed to be divine.

(2) Jesus performed miracles.

(3) Jesus' disciples believed he had risen from the dead.

(4) Jesus was crucified under Pontius Pilate, in Palestine, during the Passover.

(5) The earth was darkened on the day of Jesus' crucifixion.

(6) The primitive Church rejected polytheism.

---

196 Thallus' naturalistic explanation "was unreasonable, of course, because a solar eclipse could not take place at the time of the full moon, and it was the time of the paschal full moon when Christ died." Norman Geisler. *Christian Apologetics*. 324.

197 The New Testament details these accusations as they fell from the lips of the Pharisees: Mk. 3:22 and Jn. 8:41.

(7) Nero, among other Roman rulers, persecuted the Christian Church.

(8) The Jews accused Jesus of being illegitimate, affirming at least that Joseph was not his real father, and further attributed his miracles to Satan.

(9) The ministry of Jesus of Nazareth was during the reign of Tiberius Caesar.[198]

Albright's confirmation of the trustworthiness of the New Testament concludes our examination of the veracity of the New Covenant:

The excessive skepticism shown toward the Bible by important historical schools of the eighteenth and nineteenth centuries, certain phases of which still appear periodically, has been progressively discredited. Discovery after discovery has established the accuracy of innumerable details and has brought increased recognition to the value of the Bible as a source of history.[199]

By means of accepted principles of textual and historical analysis, the New Testament is an accurate reconstruction of the autographs — beyond reasonable doubt — as primary source documentation for the person and work of Jesus Christ.[200] Montgomery adds a summary capstone: "What, then, does a historian know about Jesus Christ? He knows, first and foremost, that the New Testament documents can be relied upon to give an accurate portrait of him. And he knows that this portrait cannot be rationalized away by wishful thinking, philosophical presuppositionalism or literary maneuvering."[201]

---

198   Francis Beckwith. *Baha'i*. Minneapolis, MN.: Bethany House Publishers. 1985. 50.

199   William F. Albright. *Christianity Today*. 18 January. 1963.

200   John Warwick Montgomery. *The Shape of the Past*. 138-39.

201   Montgomery. *History and Christianity*. 40.

CHAPTER FOUR

THE RESURRECTION OF JESUS CHRIST — BEYOND REASONABLE DOUBT?

*"And if Christ has not been raised, your faith is futile;
you are still in your sins. Then those also who have
fallen asleep in Christ are lost. If only for this life we have hope
in Christ, we are of all people most to be pitied"*
— 1 Corinthians 15:17-19.

"And if Christ has not been raised, your faith is futile..."
— John W. Montgomery boldly asserts that from its beginning,
"Christian faith has not been afraid of testability —
or of its mirror image, falsifiability."[202]

---

202 John Warwick Montgomery. *Tractatus Logio-Theologicus.* 3.611. 100.

JURISPRUDENCE & APOLOGETICS

"The interrelations of law and theology are multifarious, and one of the most striking lies at the point of conjunction in the apologetic task."[203]

The value of jurisprudence in apologetics is articulated, in principle, by analytical philosopher, Stephen Toulmin of Leeds:

One last preliminary to break the power of old models and analogies, we can provide ourselves with a new one. Logic is concerned with the soundness of the claims we make — with the solidity of the grounds we produce to support them, the firmness of the backing we provide for them — or, to change the metaphor, with the sort of "case" we present in defense of our claims. The legal analogy implied in this last way of putting the point can for once be a real help.

So let us forget about psychology, sociology, technology and mathematics, ignore the echoes of structural engineering and "collage" in the 'grounds' and 'backing,' and take as our model the discipline of jurisprudence. Logic (we may say) is generalized jurisprudence. Arguments can be compared with lawsuits, and the claims we make and argue for in extra-legal contexts with claims made in the courts, while the cases we present in making good each kind of claim can be compared with each other. A main task of jurisprudence is to characterize the essentials of the legal process: the procedures by which claims-at-law are put forward, disputed and determined, and the categories in terms of which this is done. Our own inquiry is a paral-

---

203 Montgomery. *The Law Above The Law*. Minneapolis, MN: Bethany House Publishers. 1975. 84

lel one: we shall aim, in a similar way, to characterize what may be called 'the rational process,' the procedures and categories by using which claims-in-general can be argued for and settled.[204]

Legal reasoning is synthetic and therefore "operates on probabilities, not possibilities: preponderance of evidence in most civil actions; evidence beyond reasonable (not beyond 'all') doubt in criminal matters."[205] As applied to apologetics, "the modern man faced with legally grounded evidence for Christ's claims is in the awkward position of having to go to the Cross or throw away the only accepted method of arbitrating ultimate questions in society."[206]

Further, Christian historiography entreats investigation of its truth-claims through the use of "accepted techniques of historical analysis."[207] Professor Montgomery further comments:

> Now if you are not inclined in the direction of Christianity — as I was not when I entered university — the most irritating aspect of the line of argumentation that I have taken is probably this: it depends in no sense on on theology. It rests solely and squarely upon historical method, the kind of method all of us, agnostics, or Tibetan monks, have to use in analyzing historical data.[208]

Thus, the rabbinic lawyer and Apostle of Jesus Christ, Paul of Tarsus, confronted the Stoic philosophers of Athens in offering the gospel "as the historically verifiable fulfillment of natural

---

204 Stephen Edelston Toulmin. *The Uses Of Argument.* Cambridge: The University Press, 1958. 7. In John Warwick Montgomery. Ed. *Jurisprudence, A Book Of Readings.* Strasbourg, France: International Scholarly Publishers. 1974. 271.

205 John Warwick Montgomery. *Human Rights & Human Dignity.* 153.

206 Montgomery. *The Law Above The Law.* 89-90.

207 Montgomery. *Human Rights & Human Dignity.* 134.

208 Montgomery. *Where Is History Going?* 53-54.

religion and of the natural law tradition,"[209] with the apparent assumption of the self-interpreting nature of historical facts.[210]

OPENING ARGUMENTS

The esteemed 19th century jurist, Simon Greenleaf, Royall professor of law at Harvard and the world's greatest authority on the Laws of Evidence (Greenleaf's *Laws of Evidence* was the standard textbook in English-speaking law-schools of the world for many years) challenges reasonable people: "All that Christianity asks of men on this subject, is, that they would be consistent with themselves, that they would treat its evidences as they treat the evidences of other things; and that they would try and judge its actors and witnesses, as they deal with their fellow men, when testifying to human affairs and actions, in human tribunals."[211]

The legal cross-examination of Jesus' disciples will demonstrate, beyond reasonable doubt: (1) the New Testament, particularly the Gospels and the corpus of Paul's writing, especially 1 Cor. 15, perspicuously reveals the historical bodily resurrection of Jesus Christ. And (2) the Resurrection vindicates Christ, the Son of Man, as God's Messiah — Yahweh has come in the Person of Jesus of Nazareth to renew his covenant.[212]

The Resurrection is the *sine qua non* for the symbolic world of the Gospel – 1 Cor. 15:3-8 is a clear, concise, and compelling revelation of the essence of the Gospel. In the "Tradition" (15:3)

---

209 Montgomery. *Human Rights & Human Dignity*. 133.

210 Acts 17:18-19; 22-23; 30-31. Professor Montgomery notes (Ibid. 292): "The late classical scholar E.M. Blaiklock of the University of Auckland, New Zealand, in delivering the Annual Wheaton College Graduate School Lectures, 21-22 October 1964, on the subject of Paul's Areopagus address, noted that Paul ignored the Epicureans ('the Sadducees of the Greeks'), doubtless because of the intellectual dishonesty into which their movement had fallen, and concentrated on the Stoics, who continued to hold a high view of natural law."

211 Simon Greenleaf. *The Testimony of the Evangelists*. Grand Rapids, MI.: Baker Book House. Reprint, 1984. 46.

212 See Appendix Four for biblical revelation and explanation of "The Abrahamic Covenant – It's Full-Thrust."

— "*For what I received I passed on to you as of first importance,*" Paul speaks of the universal belief among the earliest Christians that Jesus Christ was raised bodily.[213]

The Apostle brings before the bar of Jewish and pagan unbelief witnesses to the Resurrection: "*He appeared to Peter, and then to the Twelve. After that, he appeared to more than five hundred of the brothers at the same time, most of whom are still living, though some have fallen asleep. And then he appeared to James, then to all the apostles, and last of all he appeared to me also, as to one abnormally born*" (1 Cor. 15: 3-8). In each of these postmortem "appearances" Paul implies Jesus' physical, bodily resurrection. The verb translated four times "appeared" (Greek: *ophthe*) is passive indicating the Lord himself initiated the appearances; "he *actually* appeared" to his disciples.[214]

The historical, physical reality of Christ's resurrection is in full view by Paul — he "was raised" and he "was seen" — the resurrection of Jesus from the dead was not a form of "spiritual" existence — just as he was truly dead and buried, so he was truly raised from the dead bodily and seen by a large number of witnesses on a variety of occasions.

When did Paul receive the "Tradition"? Scholarly consensus dates Jesus' crucifixion at A.D. 30. And Paul's conversion is dated (also by scholarly consensus) between A.D. 31 and 33.[215]

Following his conversion, Paul went into the Arabian desert for three years; afterward, he visited Peter and James in Jerusalem; "*Then after three years, I went up to Jerusalem to get acquainted with Peter and stayed with him fifteen days. I saw none of the other apostles — only James, the Lord's brother*" (Gal. 1:18-19). Paul uses the Greek

---

213 Paul testifies that the other apostles were currently preaching the same message as he was regarding the bodily resurrection of Christ — 1 Cor. 15:9-11, 14-15.

214 Gordon Fee. *The First Epistle to the Corinthians.* Grand Rapids, MI.: Eerdmans Publishing Company. 1987. 728.

215 Gary R. Habermas & Michael R. Licona. *The Case for the Resurrection of Jesus.* Grand Rapids, MI.: Kregel Publishing. 2004. 261. Endnote #25.

term, *historesai* meaning: "to get information from"[216] to describe his visit with Peter. In the context of Galatians 1:18, the term carries the meaning: "to gain a historical account;" the implication is that Paul received the Tradition during his visit to Peter and James. Paul affirmed that the most prominent among the apostles agreed on the content of the Gospel (Gal. 1:16-2:10). Paul was then well aware of Peter's and James' beliefs, and he would therefore have been aware if the Tradition was their belief.

Perhaps Paul did not receive the Tradition (or Creed) during his trip to Jerusalem, described in Galatians 1:17-18. Habermas and Licona suggest that perhaps Paul "received it in Damascus at the time of his conversion (which places the origin of the creed even earlier). Either way he received it within two to five years after Jesus' crucifixion from the disciples themselves."[217] The importance of when Paul received the Tradition (or Creed) cannot be underestimated: *The dating of the Tradition (or Creed) means that there is no time for legends to develop concerning the resurrection – the church has always believed that on the third day Christ was raised, bodily.* The reader will observe: "On the third day" points to ordinary history (*historie*); and "Christ was raised" points to salvation-history (*heilsgeschichte*) — ordinary history and salvation-history are inseparable (*et al.* Chapter 1).[218]

---

216 Walter Bauer. *A Greek English Lexicon of the New Testament and Other Early Christian Literature.* Chicago, IL.: The University of Chicago Press. Second Edition Revised and Augmented by: F. Wilbur Gingrich and Frederick W. Danker. 1979. 383. BADG renders: ιστορησαι (*historesai*) means "To get information from."

217 Gary R. Habermas & Michael R. Licona. *The Case for the Resurrection of Jesus.* 261, endnote #25. Habermas and Licona also consider the possibility that Paul received the Tradition at an even later date. But "this could have been no later than 51, since Paul visited Corinth around that time. First Corinthians, in which Paul said that he delivered the creed to them (1 Cor. 15:3), was probably written between 53 and 57. Thus, Paul says he delivered the creed to the Corinthians when he saw them (51 or earlier) and that he received the creed earlier ("I delivered to you... what I also received"). If Peter and James were aware of the creed, it would have originated earlier still.

218 It follows from this observation, apologetics do not give access to the understanding (or experience) of the Resurrection; rather faith gives access: "That if you confess with your mouth, 'Jesus is Lord,' and believe in your heart that God raised him from the dead, you will be saved. For it is with your heart that you believe and are justified, and it is with your mouth that you confess and are saved (Romans 10:9-10).

CROSS EXAMINING THE WITNESSES

The New Testament is direct documentary evidence (primary-source evidence) for the life, death and resurrection of Jesus Christ — *Did the disciples perjure themselves in their claims to having been eyewitnesses of Jesus' historical resurrection from the dead?*

A legal construct used for the purpose of exposing perjury will be used for the cross-examination of the disciples of Jesus and their claim to having been witnesses of Christ's resurrection from the dead. The legal construct is designed to expose internal and external defects in the witnesses themselves and internal and external defects in their testimony. The legal construct for exposing perjury is illustrated below:[219]

A Construct for Exposing Perjury

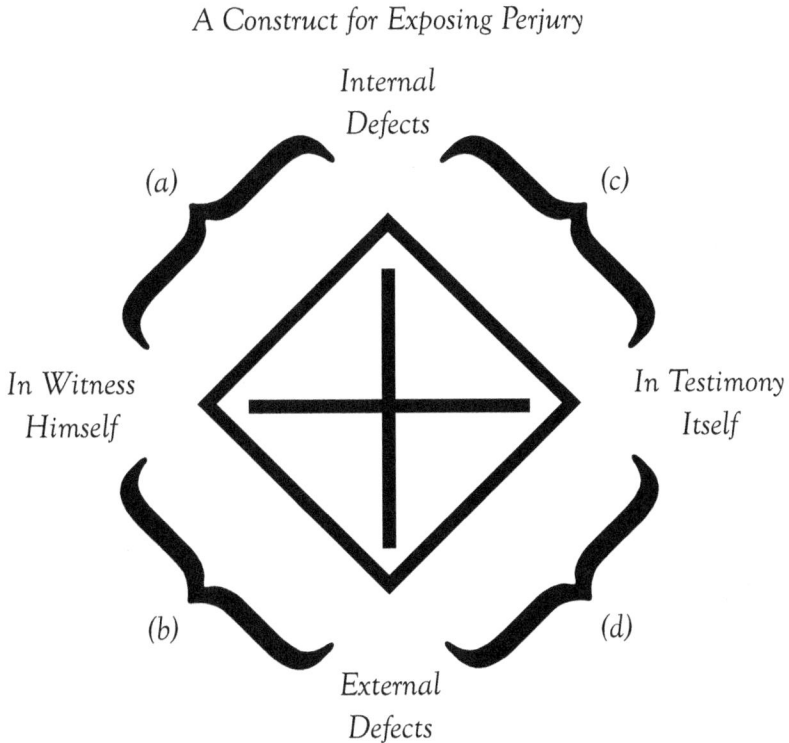

Internal
Defects

(a)   (c)

In Witness   *In Testimony*
Himself   *Itself*

(b)   (d)

External
Defects

---

219   John Warwick Montgomery. *Human Rights & Human Dignity.* Figure 5, "A Construct for Exposing Perjury." 141. The legal construct was developed by Patrick L. McCloskey and Ronald L. Schoenberg. *Criminal Law Advocacy.* Vol. 5. New York: Matthew Bender. 1984, 12.01 [b].

DO INTERNAL DEFECTS
EXIST IN THE WITNESSES?

Internal defects in the witness "refer to any personal characteristics or past history tending to show that the witness is inherently untrustworthy, unreliable or undependable."[220] Unless a motive for lying can be established, individuals are usually presumed to be telling the truth; this is a universal presumption applied in courts of law, even when the integrity of the witness is questionable.[221] It is important to again stress the significance of the presence of hostile witnesses (the plaintiffs): "The functional equivalent of cross-examination, in the case of the New Testament witnesses, was the Jewish religious community and especially its leadership, who had the means, the motive, and the opportunity to refute what the witnesses were saying about Jesus had it been false."[222]

Regarding *means*, Dr. Montgomery states: "The life of Jesus was an open book, the events of which took place within the purview of the Jewish community of the time; and Jesus' disciples followed his instruction to preach 'first to the Jew' — going first to the Synagogues, where they encountered the very religious leaders who opposed Jesus."[223] Montgomery continues by speaking of *motive* — In spite of being divided among themselves on many fronts, the Pharisees and Sadducees were united in their commitment to effect Jesus's execution; "it is therefore unthinkable that they would not have refuted inaccurate or false claims about him from their own knowledge."[224]

The knowledge possessed by Jewish leadership included their thorough awareness of Old Testament prophecy; would they [the

---

220 Ibid.

221 Simon Greenleaf. *The Testimony of the Evangelists.* 31-32.

222 John Warwick Montgomery. *Tractatus Logico-Theologicus.* 3.452. 92.

223 Ibid. 3.4521. 92-93.

224 Ibid. 3.4522. In his comments regarding Jewish leadership, Dr. Montgomery references, J. Imbert, *Le Procès de Jésus.*

Pharisees and Sadducees] not have quickly reacted to claims of ful-filled prophecy in Jesus' life made by the disciples, e.g., his birth at Bethlehem, his family's flight to Egypt, his betrayal at the hands one of his disciples for thirty pieces of silver, etc., if those claims were even slightly in error?[225] And regarding *opportunity* Montgom-ery observes that, "as community leaders, they had the ear of the public; as literate clergy, they were in an ideal position to memo-rialise for posterity any fabrications in the testimony of the early witnesses to Jesus' career"[226] — But no word of refutation is heard from the Jewish antagonists.[227]

Perhaps, contend some, the destruction of Jerusalem in A.D. 70 is a reason for the silence of Jewish opposition. But Jewish writings have survived such devastating destruction — "The early Christian witnesses preached the same message in Jewish settle-ments throughout the Roman world (the Jews of the Diaspora, *nota bene*, were not rendered mute by the Fall of Jerusalem);"[228] moreover, "... there exists no reference to lost or destroyed refuta-tions — leaving the argument in a condition purely *ex silentio.*"[229]

Simon Greenleaf argues: "It is impossible to read their writings and not feel that we are conversing with men eminently holy, and of tender consciences, with men acting under an abiding sense of the presence and omniscience of God, and of their accountability to him, living in his fear, and walking in his ways."[230] The disciples were committed to lives of personal sacrifice, humiliation, lone-liness, revilement, and oftentimes lacking in sustenance. Why

---

225 Ibid. 3.45221.

226 Ibid. 3.4523. 93.

227 Ibid. 3.4524.

228 Ibid. 3.452412.

229 Ibid. 3.452413. Modern Jewish and Gentile and skeptics such as, Jewish scholar, Joseph Klausner acknowledges the impeccable character of the disciples, noting that they were much too honor-able to perpetrate a deception. Joseph Klausner. *Jesus of Nazareth.* New York: Macmillan. 1925. 414. And D. F. Strauss, refutes charges of dishonesty on behalf of the disciples, "The historian must acknowledge that the disciples firmly believed that Jesus was risen." D. F. Strauss. *Das Leben Jesu.* Darmstadt: Wissenschaftliche Buchgesellschaft. 1835. 289.

230 Simon Greenleaf. *The Testimony of the Evangelists.* 30.

wouldn't bad men rather invent a religion that was more self-serving, which is compatible with human nature and characteristic of sinister cults, instead of spreading teachings that would deprive them of any worldly pleasure? It is incredible to think that bad men would "promote the religion of the God of truth."[231]

Perhaps these witnesses were incompetent. The competence of a witness to testify in a court of law depends on "the opportunities, which he has for observing the fact, the accuracy of his powers of discerning, and the faithfulness of his memory in retaining the facts, once observed and known."[232] No historical evidence incriminates the disciples' ability to comprehend and deal with facts. Unless the objector can provide evidence to the contrary, it can be assumed that the disciples were like the rest of their contemporaries. Greenleaf cites a uniform presumption of law that people are honest, of sound mind, and ordinary intelligence until proven otherwise.[233]

Matthew was professionally trained as a tax collector to be suspicious in his dealings with people and facts, and Luke was trained in his powers of observation as a physician. And Mark and John were simply much too unlearned to construct a forgery clever enough to escape detection by their critics.

DO EXTERNAL DEFECTS EXIST IN THE WITNESSES?

Did the disciples suffer from external defects, that is, motives to falsify testimony? McCloskey and Schoenberg discuss the critical role of this legal test:

---

231 Ibid. 31.
232 Ibid.
233 Ibid.

Not all perjurers have committed prior immoral acts or prior crimes. Frequently, law abiding citizens whose pasts are without blemish will commit perjury, not because they are inherently unworthy, but because some specific present reason compels them to do so in the case at bar. Motive, then, becomes the common denominator. There is a motive for every act of perjury. The second major way in which the cross-examiner can seek to expose perjury, therefore, is to isolate the specific motive, which causes the witness to commit perjury.[234]

Proclaiming Jesus' resurrection from the dead ran contrary to all the disciples' worldly interests; nevertheless, they preached that Christ suffered a cruel death, was resurrected from the dead, and was the Savior of the world. They faced extreme opposition that resulted in the martyrdom of all but one apostle and a great number of the other disciples; regardless, they continued to claim that God had demonstrated his willingness to redeem fallen humanity through the power of Christ's resurrection.

Every conceivable motive existed for the disciples to frequently re-examine the evidentiary basis for their faith. Greenleaf contends, "It was, therefore, impossible that they could have persisted in affirming the truths they have narrated, had not Jesus actually risen from the dead, and had they not known this fact as certainly as they knew any other fact."[235]

British legal authority, J. N. D. Anderson agrees with Greenleaf and asserts the apostles would have broken under pressure had Jesus not been raised from the dead. To consider otherwise "would run totally contrary to all we know of the disciples: their ethical teaching, the quality of their lives, their steadfastness in suffering and persecution. Nor would it begin to explain their dra-

---

234 Patrick L. McCloskey and Ronald L. Schoenberg. *Criminal Law Advocacy*. Paragraph 12:03. In Montgomery. *Human Rights and Human Dignity*. 141-42.

235 Simon Greenleaf. *The Testimony of the Evangelists*. 29.

matic transformation from dejected and dispirited escapists into witnesses whom no opposition could muzzle."[236]

In his book, *Loving God*, Charles Colson, a former Watergate co-conspirator, documents the events that led to the conviction of some of the most powerful men in the world after they failed to cover-up the infamous American political scandal that was exposed in 1973.[237] Colson comments:

> With the most powerful office in the world at stake, a small group of hand-picked loyalists, no more than ten of us, could not hold a conspiracy together for more than two weeks . . . after just a few weeks the natural human instinct for self-preservation was so overwhelming that the conspirators, one by one, deserted their leader, walked away from their cause, turned their backs on the power, prestige, and privileges.[238]

What explanation, apart from having actually seen their risen Lord can be given for the undaunted courage possessed by the disciples of Jesus only days following their Lord's cruel execution? Perhaps the disciples themselves were deceived.

Three groups had *means*, that is, direct access to the tomb of Christ and the consequent *opportunity* to expose deception in the disciples' lives: the Jews, the Romans, and the disciples themselves (though, of course, the disciples' opportunity to discover their own deception was indirect).

The disciples persistently and openly preached their message of Christ's victory over death to those who were most violently opposed to the gospel, the Jewish authorities. The Jewish authorities

---

236 J.N.D. Anderson. *Christianity: The Witness of History*. Downers Grove, IL.: InterVarsity Press, 1970. 92.

237 The Watergate scandal refers to the breaking into and bugging of the Democratic National Committee offices by a group of ex-Cuban freedom fighters that were enlisted by key individuals within the Republican administration during the presidency of Richard M. Nixon.

238 Charles Colson. *Loving God*. Grand Rapids, MI.: Zondervan. 1983. 67.

had the *means, motive,* and *opportunity* to expose as fraudulent the disciples' claim of Jesus' resurrection from the dead. Regarding Jewish motives, F. F. Bruce underscores the significance of the presence of "hostile witnesses" among the hearers of the apostolic testimony:

> It was not only friendly eyewitnesses that the early preachers had to reckon with, there were others less well-disposed who were also conversant with the main facts of the ministry and death of Jesus. The disciples could not afford to risk inaccuracies (not to speak of willful manipulation of the facts), which would at once be exposed by those who would be only too glad to do so. On the contrary, one of the strong points in the original apostolic preaching is the confident appeal to the knowledge of the hearers; they not only said, "We are witnesses of these things," but also, "As you yourselves also know" (Acts 2:22). Had there been any tendency to depart from the facts in any material respect, the possible presence of hostile witnesses in the audience would have served as a further corrective.[239]

The Jewish religious establishment, the "hostile witnesses," failed to expose the disciples as frauds because they were unable to do so. If the Jewish religious leaders had produced Jesus' corpse, the disciples would have been exposed as frauds and Christianity would have ceased to be an influence in the world (1 Cor. 15:12-19).

As for the Romans, no motive can be established for their desecration of Christ's grave. The Romans collected taxes and kept peace in the Jewish state. Pontius Pilate believed Jesus of Nazareth had caused enough turmoil, and a Roman theft of Christ's body

---

239 F.F. Bruce. *The New Testament Documents: Are They Reliable?* 45-46.

99

would have created more chaos within Israel and risked the swift, unmerciful political wrath of Caesar.

As for the disciples, no conceivable motive exists for them to have taken the body of Jesus. Indeed, if they had taken the body, they would have suffered untold misery for something they knew to be false. This dispels their personal deception.

DO INTERNAL DEFECTS IN THE WITNESSES' TESTIMONY EXIST?

Four separate gospel accounts, four different vantage points, testify to the life, death, and resurrection of Jesus of Nazareth. Is it unreasonable to hold the gospel accounts in contempt because of the diversity among their individual narrations of the events of Jesus' life and ministry? Sufficient discrepancies exist among the writers of the gospels to discount allegations of conspiracy. At the same time, substantial agreement exists among the inspired authors to demonstrate that they were well acquainted with the same great historical event. Greenleaf argues:

> The discrepancies between the narratives of the several evangelists, when carefully examined, will not be found sufficient to invalidate their testimony. Many seeming contradictions will prove, upon closer scrutiny, to be in substantial agreement; and it may be confidently asserted that there are none that will not yield, under fair and just criticism.[240]

To reiterate Greenleaf's point involving alleged discrepancies: if the different gospel accounts were all the same, then the skeptic would have a case for collusion. The author's different vantage

---

240 Simon Greenleaf. *The Testimony of the Evangelists.* 33. See Gleason Archer. *An Encyclopedia of Bible Difficulties,* for exhaustive "fair and just criticism" of alleged contradictions in the Bible.

points provide us with a built-in means to cross-examine each of them.

DO EXTERNAL DEFECTS IN THE WITNESSES' TESTIMONY EXIST?

Does historical evidence outside the New Testament confirm or deny the testimony of the gospel writers? Chapter Three: "The Trustworthiness of the New Testament," places into evidence external testimony from historians, satirists, politicians, and playwrights from the first and second centuries, which served to confirm the testimony of the writers of the New Testament.

Is the testimonial evidence presented above, sufficient for us to believe, beyond reasonable doubt, that Jesus Christ is resurrected from the dead? Or to put it another way:

IS RESURRECTION A REASONABLE INFERENCE?

Regarding the Resurrection, John W. Montgomery enquires: "How much evidence should a reasonable human being require in order to establish such a fact? Could evidence ever justify accepting it?"[241]

The eighteenth-century bishop of London, Thomas Sherlock addresses this issue of immediate apologetic concern, and ultimate religious truth as follows:

> Suppose you saw a Man publickly executed, his Body afterwards wounded by the Executioner, and carry'd and laid in the Grave; that after this you shou'd be told, that the Man was come to Life again: What wou'd you suspect in this Case? Not that the Man had never been dead; for

---

241   John W. Montgomery. *Human Rights & Human Dignity.* 154.

that you saw yourself: But you wou'd suspect whether he was now alive. But wou'd you say, this Case excluded all human Testimony; and that Men could not possibly discern, whether one with whom they convers'd familiarly, was alive or no? A Man rising from the Grave is an Object of Sense, and can give the same Evidence of his being alive, as any other Man in the World can give. So that a Resurrection consider'd only as a Fact to be proved by Evidence, is a plain Case; it requires no greater Ability in the Witnesses, than that they be able to distinguish between a Man dead, and a Man alive: A Point, in which I believe every Man living thinks himself a Judge.[242]

Montgomery observes: "Phenomenally (and this is all we need worry about for evidential purposes) a resurrection can be regarded as *death followed by life*, D., then L. Normally, the sequence is reversed, thus: L., then D."[243] The evidential criteria, for the purpose of establishing the death of Jesus of Nazareth by crucifixion, is established in the primary-source documents for the Christian faith, the New Testament (Matthew 27:50; Mark 15:37; Luke 23:46; John 19:30).[244]

The Gospels, as demonstrated in Chapter Three, are primary-source evidence for the life, death and resurrection of Jesus Christ, provide an unbroken chain of testimony from the death of Jesus Christ at point A to his resurrection at point B.[245] Jesus' corpse was placed in the tomb of Joseph of Arimathea (Matt.

---

242 Thomas Sherlock. *The Tryal of the Witnesses of the Resurrection of Jesus*. London: J. Roberts. 1729. 62. In John W. Montgomery. Editor. *Jurisprudence: A Book of Readings*. Strasbourg, France: International Scholarly Publishers. 400.

243 John W. Montgomery. Human Rights & Human Dignity. 154-55.

244 An example of contrary claims to the death of Jesus of Nazareth by crucifixion is the Koran's claim that Jesus escaped death on Calvary and later was taken up into heaven alive, Surah 4:156-59. The Koran's claim, however, is not based on any direct or documentary evidence and therefore it is inadmissible as part of our discussion.

245 See Appendix Two: The Resurrection — An Unbroken Chain of Testimony.

27:57). The tomb of Christ was sealed by the Jews and the Romans and guarded by the Romans at the request of the Jews.

Who had access to the tomb, i.e., means and opportunity?
The Romans, the Jews and the disciples had access. It has already
been argued that no motive for the removal of the body from the
tomb can be established for any of these three groups.

On the third day, following his death by crucifixion, Jesus appeared to his disciples and ate with them. Montgomery observes:

> Thus, the eating of fish is sufficient to classify the eater
> among the living, and a crucifixion is enough to place the
> crucified among the dead. In Jesus' case, the sequential
> order is reversed, but that has no epistemological bearing
> on the weight of evidence required to establish death or
> life. And if Jesus was dead at point A, and alive again at
> point B, then resurrection has occurred: *res ipsa loquitur.*[246]

Although the "secret" of life or the occurrence of death may
not be fully explicable, we have no difficulty in determining evidential criteria that places a person in one category rather than
the other. The public, unbroken chain of events, re: Appendix
Two, leads to the self-evident — *res ipsa loquitur* — verdict that the
resurrection of Jesus Christ is a reasonable inference and that any
conclusion to the contrary is to be considered unreasonable by
honest men.

CLOSING ARGUMENTS

The disciples did not perjure themselves as demonstrated by the
McCloskey-Schoenberg legal construct. Rather, these men testi-
fied "to that which they had carefully observed and considered
and well knew to be true."[247]

---

246   John W. Montgomery. *Human Rights & Human Dignity.* 155.
247   Simon Greenleaf. *The Testimony of the Evangelists.* 31.

If men are willing to be consistent with themselves, and weigh the evidence for the Resurrection as they weigh the evidence for other things; and judge the subjects and witnesses (the disciples) in the same manner they judge their fellow men when testifying to human affairs and actions in (virtually) any court of law, they will conclude, beyond reasonable doubt, Jesus of Nazareth is risen from the dead.

The Resurrection vindicates the Son of Man as God's Messiah — Jesus Christ is (beyond reasonable doubt) the divine, apocalyptic Son of Man in whom the kingdom of God has come and is coming! And therefore, humanity is no longer in exile; our sins are forgiven, and Yahweh's divine Son has entered human history to not only renew the covenant with Israel, but to restore its universal thrust to all nations (cf. Genesis 12: 1-3/Matthew 4:17/Daniel 7:13-14).[248]

POSTSCRIPT: REVELATION FROM OUTSIDE THE WORLD — THE RISEN LORD'S TESTIMONY

"The consequences of Jesus' resurrection from the dead are momentous: they include, inter alia: reasonable belief in the other miracles he performed, acceptance of his claim to Deity, a Trinitarian view of God, and a solid basis for revelational truth."[249]

The foremost evidence for the divine authority of the Bible is founded on the testimony of the risen Lord, Jesus Christ. The

---

248 See Appendix Four: "The Abrahamic Covenant — Reversing the Effects of the Fall."
249 John Warwick Montgomery. *Tractatus Logico-Theologicus.* 3.7. 112.

case for the authority of the Bible involves an inductive argument: (1) the New Testament documents are historically reliable and therefore, they are primary-source documents for the life, death and resurrection of Jesus Christ; (2) in those same primary-source documents, Jesus of Nazareth claims to be God incarnate (Jn. 2:18-22; Mt. 12:38-41); (3) in all four Gospels, Christ's bodily resurrection is described in detail — Christ's resurrection is the ultimate attestation to His deity; (4) *a priori* attempts to discredit the claims of Christ on the grounds that miracles are impossible are both scientifically and philosophically irresponsible;[250] (5) it follows, that: *"If Christ is God, then He speaks the truth concerning the absolute divine authority of the Old Testament and of the soon-to-be-written New Testament; concerning His death for the sins of the world; and concerning the nature of man and of history."*[251]

Thus, the evidentiary case[252] for the divine authority of Scripture rests on the testimony of the risen Lord. Jesus Christ quoted the Old Testament, both directly and indirectly, confirming His view of its authority. In the Sermon on the Mount (Mt. 5:17-19), Jesus affirmed the infallibility of the Old Testament: "So long as heaven and earth endure, not a letter, not a stroke, will disappear from the Law until all that must happen has happened" (see also, Jn. 10:34-35).[253]

Jesus considered the entire breadth of the Old Testament to be the authoritative Word of God: *"This is what I told you while I was still with you: Everything must be fulfilled that is written about me in the Law of Moses, the Prophets and the Psalms"* (Lk. 24:44). Jesus not only quoted Old Testament Scriptures as inspired, but he frequently taught the truth of specific Old Testament events that are often held in contempt by skeptics (e.g., select modernists, post-

---

250 See Appendix Three: "Biblical Miracles & Skepticism."

251 Montgomery. *Where Is History Going?* 179.

252 See: Henry Campbell Black. *Black's Law Dictionary, With Pronunciations*. Fifth Edition. St. Paul, MN: West Publishing CO. 1979. 500 (under heading: Evidence Rules).

253 See Appendix Six: "The Unshakable Tradition of the Old Testament."

modernists, and post-postmodernists, or applied postmodernists, etc.) under the spell of philosophical *a prioris* that would disclaim such events (i.e., miraculous events) as part of *historie*. For example, Jesus referred to the creation of Adam and Eve (Mt. 19), the great flood in Noah's day (Lk. 17:27), the divine judgment on Sodom and Gomorrah (Lk. 17:29), Moses and the burning bush (Lk. 20:32), the miracles worked by Moses in the wilderness (Jn. 3:14; 6:32), the swallowing of Jonah by the great fish (Mt. 12:4), the miracles performed by Elijah (Lk. 4:25) and the rejection of the Old Testament prophets (Mt. 23:35).

The conviction of Jesus that these and many other Old Testament events were uncontestably *historie* is realized in the fact that Christ constantly affirmed the plain historical truth of his teaching on the authenticity of certain Old Testament events and persons. His deity, for example, is bound up with the historicity of Abraham (Jn. 8:56-59).

Repeatedly, Christ employed phrases such as, "Truly, truly, I say unto you..." or "you have heard that it was said... but I say unto you" (Jn. 3:11; Mt. 5:38-39) that not only point to His authority as the Word made flesh but also dispel any notion that the Son of God accommodated His divine pronouncements, including constant affirmations of the authority of the Old Testament, to the cultural expectations of His hearers.

Jesus not only confirmed the divine authority of the Old Testament, but He also promised the divine inspiration of the New Testament. The risen Savior and Lord is Himself the full and final fulfillment of "all things" (Lk. 21:22). He is the primary subject of the whole of the Old Testament Scriptures (Mt. 5:17, Lk. 24:27; 44; Jn. 5:39).

Jesus promised to send the Holy Spirit to His disciples. He, the Holy Spirit, would "guide them into all the truth;" "teach them everything," and "call to mind all that He had told them" (Jn. 14:26-27; 16:12-15; cf. Acts 1:21-26). The Book of Acts, authored by Luke, also the writer of the third synoptic gospel, establishes the apostolic credentials of Paul of Tarsus.

Paul's doctrine is in conformity with the other apostles and the divine authority of his writing is attested by Peter (2 Pt. 3:15-16). Under the guidance of the Holy Spirit, the apostles claim divine authority for their writings (e.g., 1 Cor. 14:37). As Jews, they regarded Christianity as a fulfillment of the Jewish faith rather than a departure from it.

They further acknowledged the inspired authority of the Old Testament — 2 Tim. 3:16 literally, refers to the Old Testament as "God breathed" from the Greek, (*theopneustos*.) In his "Biblical Inerrancy: What Is at Stake," Montgomery quotes B.B. Warfield concerning the authority of Scripture:

> We do not adopt the doctrine of the plenary inspiration of Scripture on sentimental grounds, nor even, as we have already had occasion to remark on *a priori* or general grounds of whatever kind. We adopt it specifically because it is taught us as truth by Christ and His apostles, in the Scriptural record of their teaching, and the evidence for its truth is therefore, as we have also already pointed out, precisely that evidence, in weight and amount, which vindicates for us the trustworthiness of Christ and His apostles as teachers of doctrine. Of course, this evidence is not in the strict logical sense "demonstrative"; it is "probable" evidence. It therefore leaves open the meta-physical possibility of its being mistaken. But it may be contended that it is about as great in amount and weight as "probable" evidence can be made, and that the strength of conviction which it is adapted to produce may be and should be practically equal to that produced by demonstration itself.[254]

---

254 B.B. Warfield. *The Inspiration and Authority of the Bible.* Ed. Samuel G. Craig. Philadelphia: Presbyterian and Reformed Publishing Co. 1948. 218-19. John Warwick Montgomery. "Biblical Inerrancy: What Is at Stake." *God's Inerrant Word.* Ed. J.W. Montgomery. 37-38.

Regarding this inductive argument for the authority of Scripture, Montgomery stresses that Warfield correctly observed "the evidence that Christ (God Himself incarnate) held to exactly this inerrancy view of Scripture 'is about as great in amount and weight as *probably* evidence can be made' and thus warrants conviction on our part."[255]

Dr. Montgomery's Legal-Historical Apologetics, as presented in Parts One through Three objectively prescribe the Christian worldview — Part Four fits the reader with the correct lens — "*an inerrant, perspicuous and univocal written revelation*" — for "Seeing the World Aright."

---

255 Ibid. 38.

PART 4:

'SEEING THE WORLD ARIGHT'

CHAPTER FIVE

A CHRISTIAN THEOLOGY OF HISTORY: SCRIPTURAL PRINCIPLES

"The historical validation of the Christian faith yields an inerrant, perspicuous and univocal written revelation"
— John Warwick Montgomery.[256]

The Christian conception of history is ordered by the Bible's revelation of God, Father, Son, and Holy Spirit — "as Creator, Redeemer and Sanctifier of man's historical life."[257] Biblical historiography begins with a personal and therefore, meaningful creation. A Christian theology of history then centers on the historic redemptive act of Jesus, God incarnate, and finds its ultimate fulfillment in the sanctifying final judgement of God at the Second Coming of His Son:[258]

---

256 John Warwick Montgomery. *Tractatus Logico-Theologicus*. 4. 135.
257 Montgomery. *Where Is History Going?* 32.
258 Ibid.

✝

⟶   ⟶   ⟶

CREATION   REDEMPTION   LAST JUDGMENT
God's Sovereignty   *God's Love*   *God's Restoration*
of all Things

Biblical Revelation transfuses normative understanding into the whole of the historical process – "A perspicuous revelation from outside of time has clarified the meaning of history once for all."[259] In his, *The Shape of the Past*, Dr. Montgomery discusses ten principles of Christian historiography that will serve to exposit history's meaning from its beginning at creation to its end with the return of Jesus Christ and the new heaven and earth (Rev. 21:1ff).

The following principles are divided into four categories: Metaphysical (principles 1-3); Ethical (principles 4-5); Anthropological (principles 6-8); and Redemptive (principles 9-10):

METAPHYSICAL PRINCIPLES

"(1) *The entire historical process is meaningful, for it is the result of God's creative activity and has been hallowed by God's appearance in human flesh in the person of Christ and by His death for the sins of the whole world.*"[260] Biblical Revelation enables the historian to traverse the pleroma of historical events objectively. An objective

---

259 Ibid. 140.

260 John Warwick Montgomery. *The Shape of the Past*. 145. Dr. Montgomery's development of the "Ten Principles of Historical Interpretation" in this book are merely my summary of each Principle. See *The Shape of the Past*, pages 145-152 for the full text of the "Ten Principles of Historical Interpretation."

perspective on history allows for the indiscriminate, unbiased evaluation of the meaningfulness of every event.

"(2) *The decisive event ('Kairos') in the history of mankind is the act of God in Jesus Christ, and the ultimate criterion of historical significance for other events ('kairoi') — all of which are unique — lies in their relation to the Christ-act.*"[261] The Christian conception of history is teleological and the significance of each event in the historical process is understood in terms of its relation to the sovereign purposes of God in Christ. An example, offered by Montgomery, is in order:

> The events of the French Revolution must be treated as unique, not forced into a predetermined mold (contrast Toynbee's use of Greek civilization as a model for other civilizations, and the psycho-analytic historians' use of Freudian theories as categories for historical data). In evaluating the Revolution by the great Kairos, the Christian historian will probably conclude that in spite of the many positive results of the Revolution,[262] in the long run it contributed to what Voegelin calls metastatic Gnosis: the decline of the Christian faith in Europe through the substitution of human reason and immanent values for reliance upon God's transcending grace in Word and Sacrament.[263]

"(3) *Final judgment on the historical process rests in the hands of God, not of men, and will be made manifest on the last day, when all history is brought to a close with the return of Christ.*"[264] The sovereign will of God ordains all things, providing for meaningful history and

---

261 Ibid. 146.

262 In endnote #140 (*The Shape of the Past*), Montgomery notes: "For a balanced summary of the positive contributions, see John Hall Stewart. A *Documentary Survey of the French Revolution.* New York: Macmillan. 1951. 785ff.

263 Montgomery writes, *The Shape of the Past*, endnote #141: "By 1799... although France remained nominally a Catholic country, the forces of secularism were fast making themselves felt — two outstanding examples of which tendency were the establishment of civil marriage and the legalization of divorce." (Ibid. 789).

264 Ibid.

the anticipation of "the final judgment will take place at the end of time, not within time."[265] The personal judgments of the historian bow to the judgments of God and he [the historian] humbly seeks understanding. "Once battles are over," reflects Hebert Butterfield, "... the human race becomes in a certain sense one again; and just as Christianity tries to bind it together in love, so the role of the technical historian is that of a reconciling mind that seeks to comprehend. Taking things retrospectively and recollecting in tranquility, the historian works over the past to cover the conflicts with understanding and explains the unlikenesses between men and makes us sensible of their terrible predicaments; until at the finish — when all is as remote as the tale of Troy — we are able at last perhaps to be a little sorry for everybody."[266]

ETHICAL PRINCIPLES

"(4) *There exists in the universe an absolute moral law (revealed in the Holy Scriptures and fulfilled in Christ) and an absolute ethical ideal (Agape-love of God incarnated in Christ).*"[267] By subjecting himself to the moral law of Scripture, the Christian historian "imposes upon himself an absolute standard of truth; knowing that lying is of the devil[268] he will not consciously bend the historical facts of an event such as the French Revolution to fit his theories, nor will he make his case by the clever omission of facts which do not fit his hypotheses."[269] Moreover, the "morality of the Bible also provides the Christian historian with absolute standards for the

---

265 Ibid.

266 Herbert Butterfield. *Christianity and History*. London: Collins Fontana Books. 1957. 122. In John Warwick Montgomery. *The Shape of the Past*. 146-47.

267 Ibid. 147.

268 Jn. 8:44 and Acts 5:1-11.

269 John Warwick Montgomery. *The Shape of the Past*. 147.

evaluation of historical events."[270] Montgomery stresses a climatic ethical point centering on "progress":

> Furthermore, an absolute morality and an absolute ethical ideal provide the Christian historian with something desperately needed by, but unavailable to, the non-Christian historian: a criterion of progress. Optimistic secular historians such as E.H. Carr may assert that history is no longer history if its meaning depends on "some extra-historical and super-rational power" and that "history properly so-called can be written only by those who find and accept a sense of direction in history itself; the belief that we have come from somewhere"; but without the revelation of the Super-historical in time one has no absolute criterion whatever for determining where we have come from or where we should be going.[271]

"(5) *Truth in the most real sense is to be identified with personality, not with impersonal factors or forces*"[272] — The Word *became flesh* (Jn. 1:14) — Through the womb of "the virgin" (Isa. 7:14), Incarnate Deity entered human history. As image bearers of God (Gen. 1:27)[273], we relate to "Truth" (Ultimate Reality) in personal terms — Truth naturally becomes our pursuit. But "... if anyone does not have the Spirit of Christ, they do not belong to Christ" (Rom. 8:9); and they, the "natural man" (1 Cor. 2:14) must relate to, and understand truth as *correspondence* with the created order, that is, *empirical reality* (Rom. 1:19-20) — This is, nonetheless, "public truth." That is, the facts inherent in empirical reality are objective, and therefore, they are open to all people's testing regarding

---

270   Ibid.

271   Ibid.

272   Ibid. 148.

273   The "likeness-image" of God "involves humanity's special *creation relationship* with God, which makes it possible for humanity to be a meaningful reflection of God." John F. Kilner. *Dignity and Destiny. Humanity in the Image of God.* Grand Rapids, MI: William B. Eerdmans, 2015. 114.

claims made (*et. al.* Acts 2:22). Truth for the unregenerate is *indirect* through the created order. But if the image of God is fully restored in a man or woman, through regeneration (Titus 3:5b), truth is *direct* — "The Christian holds a concrete (not abstract), personal (not impersonal) idea of truth, for Christ identified truth with Himself."[274]

Moreover, positivist historiography sources the secular historian's reduction of human history to "trends" and "forces."[275] Montgomery again points to the Enlightenment as an example of the Christian historian's resistance to writing an impersonal historical account:

> In treating the French Revolution, he will make every effort to understand and appreciate the work of each in every effort to understand and appreciate the work of each individual involved in the struggle; and he will oppose all attempts of Marxist historians (to take one obvious example) who would explain the Revolution simply in terms of competitive means of production.[276]

Butterfield reacts: "One of the most dangerous things in life is to subordinate human personality to production, to the state, even to civilization itself, to anything but the glory of God."[277] Contra positivist historiography,[278] the incorporation of all domains of knowledge, as reflected in Dr. Montgomery's Christo-centric theological model above,[279] represents a total synthesis

---

274 John 14:6.

275 John W. Montgomery, *The Shape of the Past.* 148.

276 Ibid.

277 Herbert Butterfield. *Christianity and History.* 122. In John Warwick Montgomery. Ibid.

278 The basic affirmations of positivism are that *all* genuine knowledge derived by reason and logic from sensory experience, are based on "positive" data of experience; — That is, theories that are built on positivism see the world 'as it is' (a direct correspondence between one's perception and the world is a fundamental assumption of positivism). Therefore, according to logical positivism, metaphysical propositions express truth that is not only wrong and/or false but meaningless. The French scholar, Auguste Comte, originated the term 'positivism' in the 1820s.

279 Part 2 – Theological Theory Formation: Constructing The Model.

of reality — The "epistemological vividness" of Montgomery's model provides theologians, and Christian historians, with an interpretative net.[280]

ANTHROPOLOGICAL PRINCIPLES

"(6) *Human nature is constant.*"[281] The Christian historian has the assurance that men of the past are not unlike himself, and therefore he can confidently perceive and interpret the motivations of epochal making personalities of the past.[282] Montgomery observes that "the constancy of human nature permits the Christian historian to seek patterns in human history; as Koheleth says: 'Whatever is has already been, and what will be has been before; and God will call the past to account.'"[283] The doctrine of the unity of the human race[284] dismisses the instability of various secular worldviews motivated by evolutionary theories. Montgomery provides greater insight:

> We noted earlier the dilemma of present-day secular historiography: scientific historians see the need of finding patterns in the past and yet cannot justify their patterns, and relativistic historians point up the errors of their scientific counterparts but refuse to admit the need of comprehensive historical interpretations. Here again, only the Christian view has the answer: interpretative patterns are both legitimate and desirable, for they reflect the constancy of man's nature as revealed by God's word.[285]

---

280 John Warwick Montgomery. *The Suicide of Christian Theology.* 272-73.

281 John Warwick Montgomery. *The Shape of the Past.* 148.

282 Ibid. 148.

283 Ibid. 149. Eccles. 3:15; Cf. 1:9; 6:10.

284 Gen. 1:26-27; Ps. 8:4-8; Ecclesiastes, *passim*; Acts 17:26-27; Rom. 10:12; Heb. 2:6-8.

285 John Warwick Montgomery. *The Shape of the Past.* 149.

"(7) *Fallen human nature is sinful, i.e., self-centered, and this self-cen-teredness extends to all human activities in every age.*"[286] Genesis chapter three records man's quest for personal autonomy and the overthrow of God's sovereignty. Luther described mankind as *in-curvatus in se* ("curved in upon himself"). The Christian historian fully realizes that though he is redeemed, he is not exempt from the universal indictment of sin; *incurvatus in se* applies to him as well. The regenerate man is, *simul iustus et peccator*[287] — "same-time just and sinner." And thus, the historian must take Luther's theology of the Cross into account in his work as an historian.

"(8) *Because all human decisions are made in a sin-impregnated human environment, all decisions must be evaluated historically in terms of the lesser of two or more evils.*"[288] Biblical ethics are never based on expediency and neither does the end justify the means. Nevertheless, the difference between right and wrong is often difficult to determine this side of heaven. The Christian historian acknowledges the fallenness of the world system in the decision process.

REDEMPTIVE PRINCIPLES

"(9) *To God, history is 'totum simul' — an eternal present — and in the sacrificial death of Christ on the Cross His love goes out to all men of all ages.*"[289] Professor Montgomery observes: "God's love binds together the entire human race, past, present, and future."[290]

---

286 Ibid. 149.

287 (Latin) – "*simul iustus et peccator*" is from *Luther's Theology of the Cross*. The regenerate man possesses the ability to not sin, that is, he cannot sin, though he will daily inevitably sin until the resurrection. The unregenerate man cannot not sin (the double negative asserts that the unregenerate man is in a condition of sin and therefore, everything he says or does, good or bad, is tainted by sin. See: Alister E. McGrath. *Luther's Theology of the Cross*. Oxford, UK: Basil Blackwell, Inc. 1985.

288 Ibid. 150.

289 Ibid.

290 Ibid.

"(10) *Redemption from self-centeredness takes place in the presence of Christ and is available to anyone who puts his trust in Him.*"[291]

The secular historian is enslaved to himself and the context of the time in which he lives; contrary to the personal bondage of the secular historian, "the Christian historian, having been freed from slavery to himself, is able to enter into the lives of men of the past and find the historical truths that so frequently escape secularists blinded by the self. "In the fulness of time," Scripture says, "God sent forth His Son,"[292] "... when the historian lets Christ into his heart, time's fullness becomes a reality for him as well."[293]

"DISCOVERING TRUTH" ...

*"It should not be inappropriate, therefore,
to commandeer the last paragraph of Wittgenstein's Preface
to his Tractatus – with the change of a single word:
"... the truth of the thoughts that are here set forth seems to me
unassailable and definitive. I therefore believe myself to have
found on all essential points, the final solution of the problems.
And if I am not mistaken in this belief, then the ...
thing in which the value of this work consists is that it shows
how much is achieved when these problems are solved"*

— J.W.M.[294]

---

291   Ibid. 152.

292   Galatians 4:4.

293   John Warwick Montgomery. *The Shape of the Past.* 152.

294   John Warwick Montgomery. *Tractatus Logico-Theologicus.* P. 8. As referenced by Montgomery, the last paragraph in Wittgenstein's Preface, to his *Tractatus Logico-Philosophicus* is as follows:
      "On the other hand the *truth* of the thoughts that are here communicated seems to me unassailable and definitive. I therefore believe myself to have found, on all essential points, the final solution of the problems. And if I am not mistaken in this belief then the second thing in which the value of this work consists is that it shows how little is achieved when these problems are solved."
      L.W. – Vienna, 1918.

While standing before King Hadrian (dating between 120-130 A.D.), Aristides of Athens described Christians as "... those, who more than all other ethnicities (ἔθνη) on earth, have discovered the truth."[295] "Why, we ask, should one conception of Being be preferred to another? Why should one religious view of what is ontologically real command more belief than another?"[296] And "How do we know the given answer is true?"[297] Who can answer these questions, unless, of course, they have thrown away "the ladder" and transcended Wittgenstein's propositions?

"THEN HE WILL SEE THE WORLD ARIGHT"[298]

"It follows from the preceding that all Biblical assertions bearing on philosophy of history is to be regarded as revealed truth, and that all human attempts at historical interpretation are to be judged for truth-value on the basis of harmony with Scriptural revelation"[299]

— John Warwick Montgomery's Sixth Proposition.

Biblical revelation establishes normative understanding to the whole of the historical process — "A perspicuous revelation from outside of time has clarified the meaning of history once for all."[300] John Warwick Montgomery's Legal-Historical-Apologetic, climatically concluding with his "Scriptural Principles of Historiography,"

---

295 Aristides. *Apology* 15.1. Stamenka E. Antonova. *Barbarian or Greek? The Charge of Barbarism and Early Christian Apologetics.* Series Editor Robert J. Bast. Leiden (The Netherlands): Brill. 2019. 3.

296 John Warwick Montgomery. *Tractatus Logico-Theologicus.* 2.1931. 31.

297 Ibid. 2.1932b. 32.

298 L. Wittgenstein. *Tractatus Logico-Philosophicus.* 6:54b.

299 John Warwick Montgomery. *The Shape of the Past.* 138-39.

300 Ibid. 140.

profoundly moves us to, "so to speak, throw away the ladder" and "see the world aright" in "harmony with Scriptural revelation" — **"Whereof one *can* speak, thereof one must *not* be silent."**[301]

---

301 John Warwick Montgomery. *Tractatus Logico-Theologicus.* 7.

THE 'ARGUMENT FROM CONTINGENCY'

Philosophical theists regard the "argument from contingency" for the existence of God the cornerstone of "classic proofs." During the course of his 1948 BBC debate with Bertrand Russell, the author of *Principia Mathematica* together with A.N. Whitehead, and founder of analytic philosophy along with Gottlob Frege, G.E. Moore, and his student and protégé, Ludwig Wittgenstein, F.C. Copleston, the renown historian of philosophy, exquisitely delivered the argument from contingency:

> First of all, I should say, we know that there are at least some beings in the world which do not contain in themselves the reason for their existence. For example, I depend on my parents, and now on the air, and on food, and so on. Now, secondly, the world is simply the real or imagined totality or aggregate of individual objects, none of which contain in themselves alone the reason for their existence. There isn't any world distinct from the objects which form it, any more than the human race is something apart from the members. Therefore, I should say, since objects or events exist, and since no object or experience contains within itself the reason of its existence, this reason, the totality of objects, must have a reason external to itself. That reason must be an existent being. Well, this being is either itself the reason for its own existence, or it is not. If it is, well and good. If it is not, then we must proceed farther. But if we proceed to infinity in that sense, then there's no explanation of existence at all. So, I should say, in order to explain existence, we must come

to [a] being which contains within itself the reason for its own existence, that is to say, which cannot not-exist.[302]

The argument from contingency is supported by a staggering wealth of scientific evidence. For example, "the second law of thermodynamics states that for irreversible processes in any closed system left to itself, the entropy (loss of available heat energy) will increase with time: thus the universe, viewed as such a system, is moving to the condition of maximum entropy (heat death): *but* (and this is the significant aspect of the matter ...) if the irreversible process had begun an infinite time ago — if, in other words, the universe were uncreated and eternal — the earth would *already* have reached maximum entropy."[303] But, of course, this is not the case and we can only conclude that the universe is finite; the existence of the universe must be explained by a creative power outside of itself — "In the beginning God created the heavens and the earth" (Gen. 1:1). It is appropriate to dispense with numerous mundane arguments about why God exists and assert Genesis 1:1 — Ponder the argument set-forth by Alvin Plantinga:

> We should note that the question "Why does God exist? never does, in fact, arise. Those who do not believe that God exists will not, of course, ask *why* He exists. But neither do believers ask that question. Outside of theism, so to speak, the question is nonsensical, and inside of theism, the question is never asked....
>
> Now it becomes clear that it is absurd to ask why God exists. To ask that question is to presuppose that God does exist; but it is a necessary truth that if He does, He has no cause. And it is also a necessary truth that if He has no

---

302 Quoted in: John Warwick Montgomery. "Is Man His Own God?" *Christianity for the Tough Minded.* Ed. John Warwick Montgomery. 25-26.

303 Ibid. 26.

cause, then there is no answer to a question asking for His causal conditions. The question "Why does God exist?" is, therefore, an absurdity.[304]

---

304 Alvan Plantinga. "Necessary Being." *Faith and Philosophy.* 1964. In John W. Montgomery. "Is Man His Own God?" 27.

THE RESURRECTION — AN UNBROKEN CHAIN OF TESTIMONY[305]

By means of a reconstruction of the unbroken chain of testimony from the death of Jesus Christ at point A to his resurrection at point B, as revealed in the Gospels, Appendix Two extends the argument made above: *Is Resurrection a Reasonable Inference?*

MATTHEW 28:1-2; MARK 16:1-2,9; LUKE 24:1; JOHN 20:1

While the darkness struggles to keep the first light of day from breaking through, the women visited the tomb. According to Jewish reckoning, the Sabbath ended, and the next day began at sunset, so that if the Resurrection took place before midnight, it still would have occurred on the first day of the week, the third day following Christ's burial. The following events align the four testimonies concerning the visit of the women to the tomb.

MATTHEW 28:1-8; MARK 16:1-8; LUKE 24:1-11; JOHN 20:1-2

On the morning of the first day of the week, the women visited the tomb of Jesus. Luke tells us that following the death of their Lord, the women went home and rested on the Sabbath, chapter 23, verse 56. Mark adds to this that as the sun went down and the Sabbath ended, the women prepared spices for the purpose of embalming their Lord's body. They were either unaware of Joseph's and Nicodemus' prior embalming of Jesus' body or else

---

305   Re: Part 3: Verifying Montgomery's Legal-Historical Methodology. Chapter 4: "The Resurrection of Jesus Christ — Beyond Reasonable Doubt?"

they wanted to respect their Lord in this way since what had been done before for Christ appeared to be done in haste as suggested by John 19:40-42.

The placing of Jesus in Joseph's tomb is most probably historical. Early first century tombs are often described as 'acrosolias' (i.e., "bench tombs"). Archaeological evidence indicates that such tombs were used by notables in the early first century, extending credibility to the claim that Jesus was placed in such a tomb. And further, this tomb must have been clearly marked for the graves of Jewish martyrs and holy men were revered. The disciples, as well as the women, had no thought of Jesus' resurrection and so they would have wanted to preserve his grave.

All four Gospel writers agree that the women went to the tomb early dawn or early twilight, after the break of day while darkness and light were still battling for supremacy. As the women arrive at the tomb, Mark, Luke and John tell us that the women found the great stone at the entrance of the tomb rolled away.

According to Matthew, verse 6, Christ had risen; his resurrection having been preceded by an earthquake and the rolling away of the great stone that was set in place to seal the tomb by an angel who spoke to the women, "Come here and see the place where he lay."

Matthew doesn't mention the women entering the tomb but in verse 8, he mentions them coming out of it, obviously having responded to the angel's invitation. This agrees with the other three narrators of the Gospel events who all place the women inside of the tomb where they hear the angel's testimony of Jesus' resurrection.

Matthew and Mark record the angel's instructions to the women to go and tell the disciples "He has been raised from death, and now he is going to Galilee ahead of you; there you will see him!" Luke doesn't mention this, but the women are reminded, in his account, of the Lord's own prior declaration that he would rise from death on the third day. The Gospel writers do not profess to report all that the angels said but, this does not warrant charges of contradiction among the writers. The chain continues with description of the women's return to the city and the first appearance of Jesus following his resurrection.

MATTHEW 28:7-10; MARK 16:8; LUKE 24:9-11; JOHN 20:1-2

John tells us that Mary Magdalene, after seeing the stone rolled away, ran to tell Peter and John. John does not mention angels or that Mary even entered the tomb. However, the other Gospel writers tell us the women entered the tomb, saw the angels and they went back to the city.

On their way, they met Jesus. They recognized Jesus, fell to the ground and embraced his feet and worshipped him. Where was Mary Magdalene? It is evident that she was not with the other women. She could not have already seen her risen Lord for she says to Peter and John, "They have taken away the Lord out of the sepulcher, and we know not where they have laid him." She must have left the tomb before the other women because when she speaks to Peter and John, she says nothing about the angels and after returning to the tomb, she sees the angels; it is apparent that this is for the first time. And she then repeats to them that she is grieved because of the disappearance of Jesus' body in John 20:12-13.

As the other women meet Jesus on their return to the city, the Lord says, "All hail." They then worshipped Him, as formerly described. Jesus tells them to not be afraid and to go tell his disciples that they are to go to Galilee and there they shall see him.

The women began to carry out Jesus' charge; but when they conveyed these things to the disciples, they, "thought that what the women said was nonsense, and did not believe them" according to Luke 24:11. And, according to Mark 16:11, the disciples did not believe Mary Magdalene's later report of the risen Christ. The chain of testimony continues with Peter and John's visit to the tomb and Jesus' appearance to Mary Magdalene.

JOHN 20:3-18, LUKE 24:12, MARK 16:9-11

John is the only writer who gives a full account of these events because he was testifying to personal experience. Following Mary Magdalene's frantic report of the missing body to Peter and John, the two apostles run to the tomb. John outruns Peter and arrives at the tomb first. John stoops down and sees the grave clothes but does not enter. Peter finally makes it to the tomb, and he enters it and sees the grave clothes lying together, in an orderly fashion; but the napkin that was on the Lord's head was neatly folded in a place by itself. John steps inside the tomb "and he saw and believed."

Thieves had not entered the tomb, for the garments and spices would have been more valuable to them than a naked corpse. And thieves would not have taken the time to fold the grave clothes and neatly arrange the napkin. But what about the Lord's friends; his friends would not have left the grave clothes behind. These self-evident truths impressed the heart of John — "he saw and believed." John began to recall Jesus' announcement that he would rise again from the dead; a declaration the Jews took *seriously*, so they acted to set a watch at the tomb.[306]

It is noteworthy that no evidence exists for any claim that the disciples fled to Galilee, and this also implies that they were in Jerusalem and therefore, their visit to the empty tomb is very plausible. Further, it would have been impossible for the disciples to proclaim the resurrection of Jesus Christ from the dead had the

---

306 Matthew 27:62-66.

tomb not been empty. The earliest Jewish explanation was an attempt to explain the empty tomb: "His disciples came during the night and stole him away." This is persuasive evidence attesting to Jesus' empty tomb over against nonsensical and godless inventions such as, "his body was thrown into the criminals' graveyard and eaten by dogs."[307]

Mary Magdalene had followed Peter and John back to the tomb. Mary weeps in her grief as she, like John, stoops to look inside the tomb. She sees two angels, one at the head and one at the foot of where Jesus had laid. The angels ask why she is weeping, and she tells them, "Because they have taken away my Lord, and I know not where they have laid him."[308] After saying this to the angels, Mary turns around and sees a Man whom she fails to recognize; she thinks he is the gardener. He also asks her, "Why are you crying?" She again expresses her grief over not knowing where the body of her Lord is. And he speaks her name, "Mary!" The truth of her Lord's resurrection fills her soul, and she exclaims, "Rabboni!" – "My dearest Master!"

The chain continues with Jesus' appearances to the two disciples on their way to Emmaus and to Peter.

LUKE 24:13-35; MARK 16:12-13; and 1 CORINTHIANS 15:5

This is a scene wherein two disciples are journeying from Jerusalem to Emmaus, following their Lord's death and on the morning of the first Easter. One of these two disciples, Cleopas, was among those men who did not believe the reports of the women, Luke 24:25. It is noteworthy that people were no more given to belief

---

307 John Dominic Crossan. *Who Killed Jesus? Exposing the Roots of Anti-Semitism in the Gospel Story of the Death of Jesus.* San Fracisco, CA: Harper Collins. 1995.

308 John 20:13b.

without evidence in the first century than they are in our century; unless, perhaps, they were even less gullible than our culture!

Paul describes Jesus' appearances to the Apostles. Thomas is absent at the first appearance, but he is present for the second appearance, following in the chain of events below.

MARK 16:14; LUKE 24:36-48; JOHN 20:19-29; 1 CORINTHIANS 15:5

Luke gives the fullest account of our Lord's first appearance to His disciples; John describes a few circumstances; Mark and Luke both preserve the charge from Jesus to preach the gospel throughout the world.

When Paul says the Lord appeared to the twelve, he is referring to the usual designated number of the disciples and very likely this designation applies to both occasions. Mark and Luke speak of eleven disciples present but John tells us Thomas was absent for the first appearance of Christ to the disciples and so, there were ten.

According to Mark, the disciples were eating their evening meal. John says the doors were shut for fear of the Jews. And suddenly, Jesus came and stood amid His disciples and said, 'Peace be unto you!'

When Thomas is again present with the rest of the disciples, they tell him how the Lord appeared to them. But Thomas will not believe the other disciples just as the disciples refused to believe the women. Thomas tells the other disciples that "except I shall see in his hands the print of the nails and put my finger into the print of the nails, and thrust my hand into his side, I will not believe."

Eight days later, when the disciples, including Thomas, are all assembled, the Lord graciously appears to them. Jesus permits Thomas to examine his scares, as he demanded and charges him to not be faithless but believing. Thomas joyfully exclaims, "My Lord and my God!" Thomas recognizes that Christ is incarnate Deity.

Jesus says to his doubting disciple: "Thomas, because you have seen me, you have believed; blessed are those who have not seen and yet have believed!" Thomas and the other disciples who were called to be the heralds of the Gospel, the Resurrection of Jesus Christ and the hope of eternal life, refused to believe apart from empirical evidence. And yet, all others who follow the original disciples believe based primarily on their testimony. God has overruled their unbelief and made the Gospel a powerful testimony to the world through them. The Lord's appearance in Galilee to his disciples is another link in the chain of events.

JOHN 21:1-24; MATTHEW 28:16-20; 1 CORINTHIANS 15:6

While the disciples are still in Jerusalem, the Gospel narrative of Matthew records (26:32) the appointment of a time by Jesus for his disciples to meet him in Galilee on a certain mountain. Sometime after Jesus' two appearances to them in Jerusalem, they left from there and returned to Galilee, their home. While waiting for the appointed time, they involved themselves in their vocation of fishing. John speaks of seven of them being together, fishing all night but failing to catch anything. At early dawn, Jesus appeared to them on the shore and called to them to cast their net on the right side of the boat. They did so, but because of the multitude of fish they caught, they could not pull the net back into their boat.

The disciples recognized that this was a miracle granted to them by their Lord. And they started for shore. Peter, in his typical impetuous manner, jumped overboard and began swimming to Jesus. Jesus told them to prepare a meal from their fresh catch. And he, Jesus, ate bread and fish with them.

Finally, the appointed time to go to Galilee and meet the Lord there arrived. The disciples returned to Galilee, to the mountain where Jesus told them to go. It appears that not only were the eleven present but also the five hundred mentioned by Paul, 1 Corinthians 15:6. Even here, in Galilee, some doubted.[309] Most probably, the eleven were not among the doubters after all that they had experienced. The Lord's final appearances in Jerusalem and the description of his ascension complete the links in the chain of testimony.

1 CORINTHIANS 15:7; ACTS 1:3-12; LUKE 24:49-53; MARK 16:19-20

Luke tells us — Acts 1:3, that Jesus showed himself alive to his apostles, "after his passion, by many infallible proofs, being seen of them forty days, and speaking of the things pertaining to the kingdom of God."

CONCLUSION

This textual reconstruction of unbroken testimony leads to the self-evident res *ipsa loquitur* conclusion of Jesus Christ's resurrection from the dead.

---

309 Matthew 28:17.

BIBLICAL MIRACLES & SKEPTICISM[310]

Did the resurrection of Jesus Christ from the dead *actually* occur? An affirmative response to this question requires a supernatural explanation. Skeptical obstacles, however, stand in the way of such explanations. Professor Montgomery points to the modern origins of these obstacles to the reality of miracles:

> Since the rise of modern secularism in the 18th-century "Enlightenment," arguments have been put forward to limit the range of happenings to the "natural" (as opposed to the supernatural or miraculous). Commonly these arguments are based upon an assumption as to the character of the Natural or physical laws that everywhere apply.[311]

Therefore, science is often appealed to as an exploder of Christian claims to the miraculous; science studies the *regularities* of the universe (i.e., natural laws), and since the rise of modern secularism, natural laws are considered immutable. Consequently, the positivist view of science *assumes* that natural laws *prescribe* how the universe *must* operate (i.e., the universe is assumed to be a closed system and therefore it cannot be imposed upon by any external power); causality in the universe is therefore limited to secondary causes.

How do we then find our way in search of a "supra-empirical" God and Savior? Dr. Montgomery asserts:

> Historical investigation very definitely can take place on the empirical level without the positivistic presupposition that the nexus of natural causes cannot be broken. It seems

---

310 Re: "Verifying Montgomery's Legal-Historical Methodology." Chapter 4: "The Resurrection of Jesus Christ — Beyond Reasonable Doubt?"

311 John Warwick Montgomery. *Principalities and Powers*. 43.

to me that the question here is whether historical method, apart from that rationalistic presupposition, will or will not yield revelatory data concerning Jesus Christ. And if one says that it won't, then one strips away the meaning of the word "objectivity."[312]

Professor Montgomery contends that empirical method, as applied to historical investigation, will lead to supernatural inferences regarding ultimate Christian truth-claims:

The gospel events, if they can in fact be shown to have occurred, require an answer to Jesus's straightforward question, "But who do you say that I am?" (Matt. 16:15). Now, as then, only one answer will fit the facts.

Montgomery continues:

And it should be noted with care that once the facticity of Christ's resurrection has been granted, all explanations for it reduce to two: Christ's own (He rose because He was God) and any and every interpretation of the event is contradiction to this explanation. Surely it is not difficult to make a choice here, for Jesus (unlike anyone else offering an explanation of the Resurrection) actually arose from the dead! His explanation has *prima facie* value as opposed to those in contradiction to it, presented as they are by persons who have not managed resurrections themselves. The very fact that a miracle is a nonanalogous event offers an even greater reason than ordinarily to let it interpret itself, to seek its interpretation within itself. What other event or interpreter, after all, could help us understand it? But when we do go to the One who personally experienced the Resurrection, all gratuitous interpretations of the chariot-

---

312 Montgomery. *Where Is History Going?* 228.

of-the-gods, creature-from-outer space variety evaporate in the light of His own clear affirmation of His divine character, to which the sign of Jonah unequivocally points.[313]

Montgomery's reasoning confronts the skeptic — the skeptic is unjustified in his rejection of the primary-source documents of the Christian faith merely because they contain descriptions of miraculous events. On the contrary, any *a priori* bias of the investigator, e.g., historian, scientist, theologian, etc., must yield to the evidence uncovered by means of open-minded historical investigation of any event, unique or otherwise.[314]

HUME'S ENQUIRY

The Enlightenment of the eighteenth century set the stage for the era of modern rationalism and the introduction of one of Christianity's most formidable opponents, David Hume. In his *Enquiry Concerning Human Understanding,* Hume argues against the possibility of miracles:

A miracle is a violation of the laws of nature; and as a firm and unalterable experience has established these laws, the proof against a miracle, from the very nature of the fact, is as entire as any argument from experience can possibly be imagined... unless it be, that these events are found agreeable to the laws of nature and there is required a violation of these laws or in other words, a miracle to prevent them? Nothing is esteemed a miracle, if it ever happens in the common course of nature.... There must, therefore, be a uniform experience against every miraculous event; otherwise the event would not merit that appellation. And as a uniform experience amounts to proof, there is here a

313   John Warwick Montgomery. *Faith Founded On Fact.* 62-63.
314   Montgomery. *Human Rights & Human Dignity.* 151.

direct and full proof, for the nature of the fact, against the existence of any miracle.[315]

Montgomery observes that Hume dismisses historical investigation in favor of philosophical bias because of his *a priori* commitment to the immutability of natural laws. Hume's position reduces any historical event involving the miraculous to trivia on the basis that any claim to the miraculous must presuppose the contravening of otherwise unalterable natural law. However, concession to the *prescriptive* nature of natural laws does not merely reduce the miraculous to trivia; rather miracles are then considered altogether impossible.[316]

Professor Montgomery's apologetic for the possibility of miracles follows this line of reasoning:

> I have maintained (1) that when Hume assumes that there is an "unalterable experience" against miracles and concludes that miracles do not occur, he is engaged in completely circular reasoning, and that only a truly inductive approach (examining without prejudice the firsthand evidence for alleged miracles) can ever answer the question as to whether they in fact occur, and (2) that miracles cannot be ruled out a priori in our contemporary Einsteinian universe where, in the words of philosopher Max Black, the concept of cause is "a peculiar, unsystematic, and erratic notion," so that "any attempt to state a 'universal law of causation' must prove futile."[317]

Contra the question-begging exploits of David Hume, "no one (believer or unbeliever) who lives in today's Einsteinian uni-

---

315 David Hume. *An Enquiry Concerning Human Understanding.* "Of Miracles." Indianapolis, IN.: Hackett Publishing Company. 1977. Edited by Eric Steinberg. Sec. X, Pt. I, 76-77.

316 John Warwick Montgomery. *Faith Founded On Fact.* 48.

317 Ibid. 46-47.

verse can benefit from the luxury of an absolute natural law."[318] Professor Montgomery further expounds:

> Under only one condition would Hume's argument hold, namely, if there were irrefutable evidence for the existence of a rigorous framework of natural law in the universe which would render absurd the idea of its violation. Do we have evidence? Newton thought so and so has the traditional Religion of Science. Yet, since Einstein, science has gradually given up the notion. Rather than looking at natural law as structure which is already present in the universe and which is progressively being discovered, scientists of today see natural law as the human description of what is observed to happen in the universe. Such a conception of natural law is the only truly empirical one, for it places all events, regardless of their uniqueness, on equal footing — all are to be tested for error by a study of the empirical evidence for them, not ruled out *a priori* because they have not happened as many times as other events.[319]

Abandonment of the deterministic worldview in physics has progressively moved scientists toward the understanding that natural laws are *descriptive* of the *regularities* of the universe instead of *prescriptive* of how the universe *must* operate.

Hume fails to distinguish between primary and secondary causes (opting rather for a universal causation of all phenomena) and thus, he reduces the operations of the universe to an impersonal fatalism. However, "In actuality, no one has a sufficiently comprehensive knowledge of the universe to formulate in advance 'firm and unalterable' laws of nature. We use our past

---

318   Ibid. 48.
319   John Warwick Montgomery. *The Shape of the Past.* 291.

experience as a working hypothesis — not as a 'Procrustean bed' — in investigating new or strange phenomena."[320]

Therefore, the evidence in support of an event, not philosophical *a priori*, is to be the basis for judging the fact or otherwise of an event, regardless of its uniqueness, taking place within the purview of history. The significance of a miracle is not determined by some universal framework of natural law, but rather "... its very degree of uniqueness gives strong evidence for the truth of the claim of the one who performed it and/or the claim of the book in which it is recorded."[321]

Montgomery cites Ian Ramsey for his perceptive observation:

> ... scientific regularity tends to reduce rather than heighten significance, whereas history, with its stress on the particular and the concrete, is the stuff out of which significance is made: "Scientific language may detail uniformities more and more comprehensively, but its very success in so doing means that its pictures are more and more outline sketches of concrete, given fact.... In history we are not concerned with abstract uniformities but with a concrete level of *personal* transactions."[322]

Thus, whether "a historical miracle will be 'significant,' then will not depend on its relation to supposed natural law, but on its inherent, concrete character. If an event touches the wellsprings of universal human need, its significance can hardly be doubted."[323] Therefore, "does the Scripture refer to even the least redemptive

---

320 Montgomery. *Principalities and Powers.* 45.

321 Ibid. 292.

322 Ian Ramsey. "Miracles: An Exercise in Logical Mapwork." *The Miracles and the Resurrection.* ("Theological Collections," 3; London: S.P.C.K., 1964). 7,13. John Warwick Montgomery. *Faith Founded On Fact.* 51.

323 Ibid.

of Jesus' miracles as *semeia* ("signs") that point to Him and to the truth of His divine claims."[324]

David Hume's definition of miracle is in accord with his naturalistic assumption that the universe is a closed, programmed system. However, Einsteinian relativity has transformed the former Newtonian model of physics, rendering Hume's definition groundless.[325]

Rather than a "violation" of natural laws, Biblical miracles are unique, *nonanalogous* events taking place within the purview of history, having evidential value and requiring a religious explanation.[326]

CONTEMPORARY OPPOSITION TO THE MIRACLE APOLOGETIC

Philosopher Antony Flew presents a contemporary twist to the former Humean opposition to the possibility of miracles:

> The basic propositions are: first, that the present relics of the past cannot be interpreted as historical evidence at all, unless we presume that the same fundamental regularities obtained then as still obtain today; second, that is trying as best he may to determine what actually happened the historian must employ as criteria all his present knowledge, or presumed knowledge, of what is probable or improbable, possible or impossible; and third, that, since *miracle* has to be defined in terms of practical impossibility the application of these criteria inevitably precludes proof of a miracle.[327]

---

324 Ibid. 51-52.

325 John Warwick Montgomery. *The Shape of the Past*. 291.

326 Montgomery. *Faith Founded On Fact*. 50-51.

327 Antony Flew. *God & Philosophy*. London: Hutchinson. 1966. Sec. 7.10. 146. John Warwick Montgomery. Ibid. 52.

Flew appears to insist that empirical method is inadequate as a means of historical investigation, particularly concerning the occurrence of miracles. The inadequacy of empirical method is due to its inability to rise above mere probability, and consequently its potential inconsistency renders it unable to distinguish deviations from regularity. Therefore, empirical method must be considered inapplicable where the investigation of miracles is concerned.

Montgomery addresses Flew's contentions as follows:

> But here a lamentable confusion is introduced between what may be termed *formal* or *heuristic* regularity and *substantive* regularity. To investigate anything of a factual nature, empirical method must be employed. It involves such formal or heuristic assumptions as the law of non-contradiction, the inferential operations of deduction and induction, and necessary commitments to the existence of the investigator and the external world. Empirical method is not "provable." The justification for its use is the fact that we cannot avoid it when we investigate the world. (To prove that what we perceive with our senses is real, we would have to collect and analyze data in its behalf, but we would then already be using what we are trying to prove!). One cannot emphasize too strongly that this necessary methodology does not in any way commit one to a substantively regular universe: to a universe where events must always follow given patterns. Empirical method always investigates the world in the same way — by collecting and analyzing data — but there is no prior commitment to what the data must turn out to be.[328]

If empirical methodology is discounted on the grounds that it cannot yield apodictic certainty but rather only probable re-

---

328   Ibid. 52-53.

event."[334] Therefore, "... *miracles are impossible only if one so defines them — but such definition rules out proper historical investigation.*"[335]

334 Montgomery. *Faith Founded On Fact.* 57.

335 Montgomery. *The Shape of the Past.* 139.

THE ABRAHAMIC COVENANT — REVERSING THE EFFECTS OF THE FALL [336]

Scripture foresaw that God would justify the Gentiles
by faith and announced the gospel in advance to Abraham:
"All nations will be blessed through you"
— Galatians 3:8.

Now the Lord said to Abram, "Go from your country
and your kindred and your father's house to the land that
I will show you. And I will make of you a great nation,
and I will bless you and make your name great,
so that you will be a blessing. I will bless those who bless you,
and him who dishonors you I will curse,
and in you all the families of the earth shall be blessed"
— Genesis 12:1-3.

In Genesis 12:1-3, God sovereignly calls Abram into covenant relationship, that is, a mutually binding relationship between two
parties who willingly promise to faithfully live by its terms (cf.
Deut. 28-29; Lev. 26) —The *Lord* had said to Abram, "Go from
your country, your people and your father's household to the land
I will show you. I will make you into a great nation, and I will bless

---

336 Re: Part 3: "Verifying Montgomery's Legal-Historical Methodology." Chapter 4: "The Resurrection of Jesus Christ — Beyond Reasonable Doubt?" Subtopic: "Opening Arguments. Footnote
#202.

you; I will make your name great, and you will be a blessing. I will bless those who bless you, and whoever curses you I will curse; and all peoples on earth will be blessed through you."

The primary purpose of God's covenant with Abram was the reversal of the effects of the Fall of humanity (Gen. 3:1-21). The account of God's covenant with Abram begins with God promising an unbelieving, childless Abram that he would bless him with offspring equal in number to the stars in the sky (Gen. 15:1-5). Abram was 99 years-old and his barren wife, Sarai, was 90 years-old. But Abram believed God, "and he credited it to him as righteousness"[337] (Gen. 15:6).

Ancient covenants required the weaker party to prepare and offer a blood sacrifice to the stronger party. Therefore, after promising to give Abram land as his inheritance (Gen. 15:7), God tells him to bring him a heifer, a goat and a ram each three-years-old along with a dove and a young pigeon (Gen. 15:9). Abram brought the sacrifice to God and cut each of the larger animals in-half and arranged them opposite of each other. A bloody path through the sacrificed animals was created. Abram did not cut the birds in-half; he severed their heads and drained their blood, mixing it with the other animals (Gen.15:10).

Birds of prey then came down on the sacrifice, but Abram chased them away (Gen. 15:11). As the sun began to set, Abram fell into a deep sleep. And he was covered by a thick, dreadful darkness and the Lord spoke to him, "… for four hundred years your descendants will be strangers in a country not their own and … they will be enslaved and mistreated there."

However, "they will come out with great possessions," and "you will go to your ancestors in peace …." (Gen. 15:12-15). Now, as the sun has set, and the covering of darkness blankets the land,

---

337 Paul quotes Genesis 15:6 in Romans 4:3. The word translated "credited" is used by Paul to mean to: "place to one's account … credit something to someone….", BADG, 476. By faith, Abraham was justified, that is, God credited to Abraham's account righteousness by faith.

"a smoking firepot with a blazing torch appeared and passed through the pieces" — i.e., the sacrifice. (Gen. 15:17). Something of unspeakable, staggering significance takes place, the "smoking firepot with a blazing torch" — a symbolic representation of the One who led the enslaved Israelites out of "a country not their own" as a "pillar of cloud by day" and a "pillar of fire by night" (Ex. 13:21) — passes through the sacrifice while Abram is in a deep sleep!

Genesis 15:18a.: *"On that day the Lord made a covenant with Abram ...."* It is literally of eternal significance that Abram did not pass through the sacrifice, *only* God passed through. This is confounding to Jewish commentators for ancient covenants required the weaker of the two parties to identify with the sacrificed animals and swear, saying something like, "Lord, if I am not obedient to the stipulations of this covenant, may I become as this sacrifice."[338] By God passing through the sacrifice, Yahweh was literally taking Abram's place! In other words, God made Himself Abram's *substitute*. And therefore, if Abram, and his descendants — "all nations" — were not obedient to the terms of the covenant *"the Lord made ... with Abram,"* God *Himself* would become as the slaughtered sacrifice in their behalf!

Through the Holy Spirit's inspiration, the Apostle Paul tells us that regarding Jews and Gentiles everywhere, *"There is no difference ..., for all have sinned and fall short of the glory of God"* (Rom. 3:22b-23). *"There is no one righteous, not even one..."* (Rom. 3:10) — Without exception, *no* human being has been obedient to the terms of the covenant God made with Abram and "all nations" for the reversing of the effects of our historic fall (Gen. 3:1-19).

All *"have sinned;"* sin is any transgression of or lack of conformity to the law of God. John Stott's insight into our sinful

---

338 Whereas the language involved with this pronouncement is implied, curses associated with disobedience to divine covenants in the Old Testament are explicitly mentioned in: Leviticus 26:14-35; Deuteronomy 28:15-68; and Malachi 2:2.

condition is piercing: *The essence of sin is we human beings substituting ourselves for God, while the essence of salvation is God substituting himself for us: We ... put ourselves where only God deserves to be; God ... puts himself where we deserve to be.*

Deep down, in the secret, hidden levels of human existence, every human being intuitively knows something is wrong; but because of their sinful hearts (cf. Jer. 17:9), they resist turning to God and his law and instead, they are inclined to be a law unto themselves. Everyone, on some level, struggles with the reality of their fallen condition and separation from God.

During the latter part of "Second Temple Judaism" (516 BCE – 70 CE), the Jewish nation was in exile and under the dominion of a foreign ruler, Rome. To be "in exile" is to be outside the covenant and *cursed*. To be blessed, is to be placed in (or in Israel's case, to be renewed in) the covenant and for the focused presence of God to be brought *near* and fill the land and community. *Blessing* and *curse* are related to proximity in the Jewish mind; blessing is related to nearness and curse relates to remoteness.

On a Friday afternoon, outside the gates of Jerusalem, "*Christ redeemed us from the curse of the law by becoming a curse for us, for it is written: 'Cursed is everyone who is hung on a tree.' He redeemed us in order that the blessing given to Abraham might come to the Gentiles through Christ Jesus, so that by faith we might receive the promise of the Spirit*" (Gal. 3:13-14).

God in Christ literally became as the slaughtered sacrifice for us – Isa. 53:4-8:

> *Surely he took up our pain*
> *and bore our suffering,*
> *yet we considered him punished by God,*
> *stricken by him, and afflicted.*
> *But he was pierced for our transgressions,*
> *he was crushed for our iniquities;*
> *the punishment that brought us peace was on him,*

and by his wounds we are healed.
We all, like sheep, have gone astray,
each of us has turned to our own way;
and the Lord has laid on him
the iniquity of us all.
He was oppressed and afflicted,
yet he did not open his mouth;
he was led like a lamb to the slaughter,
and as a sheep before its shearers is silent,
so he did not open his mouth.
By oppression and judgment he was taken away.
Yet who of his generation protested?
For he was cut off from the land of the living;
for the transgression of my people he was punished.

He is our *substitute* and through the blood of the Cross, the curse is broken; God's salvation is a present reality for "all nations," Jews and Gentiles together — The Apostle writes: *Understand, then, that those who have faith are children of Abraham. Scripture foresaw that God would justify the Gentiles by faith and announced the gospel in advance to Abraham: "All nations will be blessed through you." So those who rely on faith are blessed along with Abraham, the man of faith* – Galatians 3:7-9.

The original thrust of the covenant (Genesis 12:1-3) has been restored — *the seed of the woman has crushed the head of the serpent* (Genesis 3:15b) and the effects of the Fall (Genesis 3:1-21) have been reversed through faith alone (*sola fides*) in Jesus Christ alone (*sola Christus*/Romans 4:25). God has reclaimed his creation in sovereign power through the Resurrection — the old creation is put to death at Calvary and new creation emerges on Easter Sunday — *The Abrahamic Covenant has reversed the effects of Genesis 3, the Fall of Mankind.*

THE PROBLEM OF EVIL

*"If you are sure that this natural world is unjust
and filled with evil, you are assuming the reality of some
extra-natural standard by which to make your judgment"*

– C.S. Lewis

The Eighteenth-Century Scottish Empiricist, David Hume, inquires, "Is God willing to prevent evil, but not able? Then is he impotent? Or is he able but not willing? Is he then malevolent? Is he both able and willing? Why is evil then?[339]

All orthodox theology hangs on two primary truths: God is *able*, and God is *willing – God is the sovereign, almighty God over all creation, visible and invisible, and God is good in all His ways.* This is the point of Hume's attack. And Hume's query, "Why then is evil?" is to imply, "Since God is the Creator of all things visible and invisible, do we then conclude that God created evil?" Regarding empiricism and vast depths of knowledge, David Hume is very formable, but concerning metaphysics (and theology), the esteemed Scottish philosopher is very vulnerable – Hume appears oblivious to man's sinful condition and hence, his moral culpability concerning evil.

---

339 Anders Kraal. *The of God In David Hume*. Cambridge University Press. 2024.

WHAT IS EVIL?

The essence of sin is we human beings substituting ourselves for God, while the essence of salvation is God substituting himself for us. We... put ourselves where only God deserves to be; God... puts himself where we deserve to be"

— John Stott.

The Fall of Humanity is a historical event recorded in Genesis 3.[340] Adam and Eve had moral freedom in the Garden. God imposed only one restriction on Adam and Eve: They were free to eat the fruit of any tree in the garden, except one: "The Tree of Knowledge of Good and Evil."

But the Serpent, that is, Satan, deceived first Eve, then Adam, into conceiving God's commandments as [too] restrictive, instead of righteous means and ends towards their ultimate freedom through knowing God and glorifying Him forever. Adam and Eve's desire for personal autonomy, unbounded freedom, to decide what is good and what is evil *for themselves* results in their transgression against God.

Once they transgressed God, they attempted to hide from Him when they heard Him entering the Garden. And the Lord God called to the couple, "Where are you?" (3:9). Now, God is both omniscient and omnipresent, He knows all, and He is present everywhere. Therefore, "Where are you?" is phenomenal language; nothing is being pointed to regarding God, rather, the question is telling us about mankind, the "crown of God's creation" (Gen. 1:27); mankind is *lost* in the sense of a broken relationship (re: *the special relationship by creation* – Gen. 1:27) with God because of sin. The image of God is still present, for "man" is referred to

---

340 The Fall of man is an *actual* historical event with metaphysical consequences, as described above.

in Scripture, as "man" after the Fall, but the *imago dei* (the image of God) in humanity is "marred" in three significant ways – Our separation *unto* God (sanctification) is reversed, we are then separated from God (Eph. 4:18), and our intimate *awareness* of God is lost (Eph. 4:17-19), and our right *standing* before God (Eph. 4:20-24), is exchanged for servitude to anyone or anything that takes the place of God in our lives.[341]

The [unregenerate] human condition brings us face to face with the problem of evil: "This is the verdict: Light has come into the world, but men loved darkness instead of light because their deeds were evil" (John 3:19).

What is evil? Augustine answers this question by first positing God is good, and the creation he has brought into being is good (Gen. 1:3-31). But if God is good, and his creation is likewise, then, what is the origin of evil? Augustine's answer is: "Evil has no positive nature; but the loss of good has received the name 'evil.'"[342] Evil is the privation of good: "The truth is that evil is not a real *thing* at all, it is simply good *spoiled* – "That is why I say there can be good without evil, but no evil without good."[343]

If evil has no existence apart from good, and therefore, it is not a thing, as is good, then how do humans commit evil acts? Augustine answers: "For when the will abandons what is above itself, and turns to what is lower, it becomes evil – not because that is evil to which it turns, but because the turning itself is wicked."[344] Thus, a person does not choose evil, as though it is a thing, but rather, they "can only turn away from the good, that is from a greater good to a lesser good (*re*: Augustine's hierarchy) since all

---

341 Regeneration (rebirth) restores these three realities to human existence and consequently we become "new creations" in the sight of God.

342 Augustine. *The City of God*. Edited: Whitney J. Oates. *Basic Writings of Saint Augustine*. Vol. Two. Grand Rapids, MI.: Baker Book House, Reprinted: 1992. XII, Ch. 9.

343 C.S. Lewis. *The Letters of C.S. Lewis to Arthur Greeves* (1914-1963). Edited by Walter Hooper. New York: Collier/Macmillan, 1986. 465.

344 Augustine. *The City of God*. XII, Ch. 6.

things are good."[345] Evil then is an illicit reach for the "Beautiful and the Good" — "And I strained to perceive what I now heard, that free-will was the cause of our doing ill."[346]

Human nature is predisposed to desire the perverse, instead of the "Beautiful," and depravity instead of the "Good" (Rom. 3:10-18; 23). But though human freedom is the source of evil, it is also the source of virtue — courage, faithfulness, and compassion (among a myriad of other human virtues) are expressed through the character of free moral beings. Therefore, although moral freedom allows for moral evil, it also allows for the greater good in our world.

Alluding to Luther's *theologia crucis* (theology of the Cross), Jürgen Moltmann penetrates to the reality of living in a world wherein what men intend for evil; God ultimately intends for good:

> Since I first studied theology, I have been concerned with the theology of the cross... It is the basic theme of my theological thought. No doubt this goes back to the period of my first concern with questions concerning Christian faith and theology in real life, as a prisoner of war behind barbed wire... Shattered and broken, the survivors of my generation were then returning from camps and hospitals to the lecture room. A theology which did not speak of God in terms of the abandoned and crucified one would not have got through to us then.[347]

John Stott agrees with Moltmann: "I could never believe in God if not for the Cross because in a world full of injustice, I could never believe in a God who could not identify with it; a God who was

---

345 Gregory Koukl. "Augustine on Evil." http://www.str.org/free/commentaries/apologetics/evil/augustine.htm Page 3 of 6 pages. Downloaded: 05/13/2004.

346 Augustine. *Confessions*. Edited: Whitney J. Oates. *Basic Writings of Saint Augustine*. Vol. One. Grand Rapids, MI.: Baker Book House, Reprinted: 1992.

347 J. Moltmann. *Dergekreuzigte Gott. Das Kreuz Chrisals Grund und Kritik christlicher Theologie*. Müchen, 4th edn. 1981. 7. Quoted in: Alister McGrath. *Luther's Theology of the Cross*. 180.

immune from it." God has not abandoned us to ourselves rather, he became flesh and lived among us; he endured suffering and moral evil as one of us and for us.[348]

CLOSING REMARKS

John Warwick Montgomery stresses that, "as Wittgenstein himself emphasized, absolute moral judgments can only be justified transcendentally; it follows that the atheist, having by definition no such absolute source of morality, is in a particularly disadvantageous position logically to offer criticism of the actions of Divinity."[349] Scripture informs us that the first humans transgressed God's will by reaching for the fruit of the 'Tree of the knowledge of good and evil" (Gen.3:1-7) — The consequences of their disobedience has been pain and death for them and their descendants (Gen. 15-19). Evil is not God's creation but instead, it is humanity's turning from the greater good, to a lesser good and exercising an illicit use of free-will.[350]

---

348 John Stott as quoted by Tim Keller. Sermon: Mark 14:53-65. Copywrite Redeemer Presbyterian Church. www.redeemer.com.

349 John Warwick Montgomery. *Tractatus Logico-Theologicus*. 4.8, 4.81.

350 Ibid. 4.82 and 4.822.

THE UNSHAKABLE TRADITION
OF THE OLD TESTAMENT

*For over 1,000 years, the works of the Masoretes
have been considered by Jews to be the most accurate reading
of the Hebrew Bible.[351]*

Under the heading, "The Trustworthiness Of The New Testament" (Part 3, Chapter 3), the scope of Dr. Montgomery's Theological Model is concluded in the sixth proposition of his outline of a Christian worldview: "It follows from the preceding [propositions 1-5] that all Biblical assertions bearing on philosophy of history is to be regarded as revealed truth, and that all human attempts at historical interpretation are to be judged for truth-value on the basis of harmony with Scriptural revelation."[352] Scriptural revelation begins, of course, with the Old Testament.

Whereas we do not possess the autographs (the originals) of the Old Testament, following the unparalleled archaeological discovery of the Dead Sea Scrolls, the reconstruction of the Old Testament autographs became much less arduous than the reconstruction of the New Testament autographs.

---

351 Paul Gibson. *Bible Questions. Info.* "Why is the Masoretic Text Important? March 2 ND. 2019. https://biblequestions.info/2019/03/02/why-is-the-masoretic-text-important/. Downloaded: 02/18/2025.

352 John Warwick Montgomery. *The Shape of the Past.* 138.

THE DISCOVERY OF THE DEAD SEA SCROLLS

A Bedouin Shepherd boy was throwing rocks, while caring for some goats in the desert by the Dead Sea. The young boy happened to throw one of the rocks into a cave whereupon he heard a shattering sound. The boy went inside the cave to investigate. He discovered that the rock he threw had hit a clay jar, and inside the jar were very old-looking parchments.

The boy's discovery led to the recovery of over a thousand ancient manuscripts in eleven caves between the years 1947-1956.[353] The caves are located near Khirbet Qumran on the northwestern shore of the Dead Sea. The scrolls were dated from around 250 BCE to 70 CE.[354] The Scrolls were evidently placed in the jars in 68 CE by an Essene community; the Scrolls were preserved in sealed jars for nearly 1,900 years.

Except for Nehemiah and Esther, all the books of the Hebrew Bible were discovered at Qumran. In some cases, several copies of the same book were found, e.g., thirty copies of Deuteronomy were discovered, while in other instances, only one copy, Ezra, was found. Some sections of these books are almost identical to the Masoretic text, which reached its final form about one thousand years later in medieval codices. And sometimes books conform to other versions of Scripture, e.g., the Samaritan Pentateuch or the Greek translation of the Hebrew Scriptures known as the Septuagint (LXX). Scrolls in the Septuagint Greek tradition (Exodus and Leviticus) and an Aramaic translation (Leviticus and Job) have also been discovered.

---

353 In his, *A Survey of Old Testament Introduction*, Gleason Archer Jr., *Appendix 4*, Inventory of The Biblical Manuscripts From The Dead Sea Caves, provides an inventory of MSS and fragments found in each of the eleven caves. Chicago, IL: The Moody Bible Institute. 1964, Revised Edition: 1974. 513-17.

354 The Dorot Foundation Dead Sea Scrolls Information and Study Center. "The Dead Sea Scrolls." https://www.imj.org.il/en/wings/shrine-book/dead-sea-scrolls. Downloaded: 02/16/2025.

Most of the scrolls were written in Hebrew, with a smaller number in Aramaic or Greek. Most of them were written on parchment, but a few scrolls were written on papyrus. The greatest number of scrolls were fragments; and only a handful were found intact. Scholars have, however, managed to reconstruct approximately 950 different manuscripts (MSS) from these fragments.

The manuscripts are approximately two thousand years old, dating from the third century BCE to the first century CE — *The discovery of the Dead Sea Scrolls in 1947 firmly established the fidelity of the Masoretic Tradition.*[355]

OLD TESTAMENT TRADITION

The proto-Masoretic represents the purest textual tradition of all — Gleason Archer Jr.[356]

The Masoretes' headquarters was in Tiberias; and the Modern Masoretic Period was between 500 to 900 CE. The Masoretes (from "masora" meaning tradition) accepted the laborious calling of editing the text and standardizing it. The resultant text of the Masoretes had vowel points added to ensure proper pronunciation. The Masoretic Text is the standard Hebrew text today.

---

355 Millar Burrows concludes: "It is a matter of wonder that through something like a thousand years the text underwent so little alteration. As I said in my first article on the scroll [Isaiah] "Herein lies its chief importance, supporting the fidelity of the Masoretic tradition." Quoted by: Josh McDowell. *Evidence that Demands a Verdict.* Vol. I. San Bernadino, CA: Here's Life Publishers. 1972, 1979. 58.

356 This sentence is a paraphrase formed from an explanation offered by Dr. Archer: "However, it should be understood that the existence of these non-Masoretic manuscript families does not necessarily mean that the proto-Masoretic does not represent the purest textual tradition of all. Nothing in the new discoveries from the Qumran caves endangers the essential reliability and authority of our standard Hebrew Bible text, as represented for example in the Kittel editions of *Biblia Hebraica.*" Gleason Archer Jr. *A Survey of Old Testament Introduction.* 42.

MANUSCRIPT FAMILIES

The Masoretes standardized the Hebrew Bible.[357]

Gleason Archer stresses that the Qumran manuscripts and fragments fit into three, possibly four, manuscript families:

(1) ... the proto-Masoretic, from which the consonantal text of our present-day Hebrew is derived; (2) the proto-Septuagintal, the Hebrew *Vorlage* (preceding model) of the original Greek translations that eventuated in the later Septuagint; (3) the proto-Samaritan, forming the basis for the later Samaritan text of the Hebrew Pentateuch (probably lacking the later Samaritan additions on the basis of sectarian bias); (4) a neutral family, standing more or less midway among the conflicting traditions of the first three families.[358]

"Within the field of textual criticism," observes John D. Barry, "the Masoretic Text is usually considered the central text because it is the best-preserved text of the Hebrew Bible. All scholarly and non-scholarly editions of Hebrew Scriptures revolve around MT, and many commentaries and introductions focus on that version."[359] Josh and Sean McDowell further argue: "The tradition of the MT [Masoretic Text] is significant for the following reasons: (1) It provided the only textual witness to the Old Testament for more than 1,000 years (ninth century AD to 1947); (2) Its internal consistency clearly attests to the care, precision, and systematic rigor with which the Masoretic scribes copied the manuscripts...; (3) The MT tradition allows the textual critic to reasonably posit a prior tradition going back to as early as 70 AD; and (4) It provides

---

357   Paul Gibson. *Bible Questions. Info.* "Why is the Masoretic Text Important? Downloaded: 02/17/2025.

358   Gleason Archer. *A Survey of Old Testament Introduction.* 41.

359   John D. Barry. Editor. "Textual Criticism of the Hebrew Bible, History of Text." *Lexham Bible Dictionary* (Lexham Press: 2016) YHWH. Footnote #8. Quoted in: Paul Gibson. *Bible Questions. Info.* "Why is the Masoretic Text Important? Downloaded: 02/17/2025.

the primary textual witness by which all other textual witnesses are measured...."[360]

The Aleppo Codex (re: Aleppo, Syria), smuggled back to Jerusalem in the 1950s, is the most accurate existing manuscript of the Masoretic text (another well-known manuscript is the Leningrad Codex of 1009). The Aleppo Codex is practically identical to the pre-Masoretic version of the biblical text that has been preserved in some of the biblical scrolls found at Qumran (When scholars compare the Dead Sea Scrolls with the Masoretic Text, such as the Aleppo Codex, they find few differences, and none of them are theological.)[361]

Gleason Archer asserts that "The Dead Sea Scroll of Isaiah (1QIsa) – [contains] the entire sixty-six chapters (150-100 B.C.). This important text belongs to the same manuscript family as the Masoretic Text (MT). Only occasionally does it favor a Septuagint (LXX) reading and most of its deviations from the MT are the result of obvious scribal lapses, for the text was rather carelessly copied...."[362] In another place, Dr. Archer continues: "One further remark should be made concerning the consonantal MT. When it is compared with such examples of the proto-Masoretic tradition as 1QIsa (which contains many 'extra' *matres lectionis*[363]), the MT obviously goes back to a pre-Maccabean recension of the Hebrew Bible[364] and points to the activity of a standardizing revision committee under official auspices, who consulted all the earliest and best manuscripts then available (no doubt including the

---

360 McDowell, Josh and McDowell, Sean. *Evidence That Demands a Verdict: Life-Changing Truth for a Skeptical World.* Nashville, TN: Thomas Nelson, 2017. 101-102.

361 Paul Gibson. *Bible Questions. Info.* "Why is the Masoretic Text Important? Downloaded: 02/18/2025.

362 Gleason Archer Jr. A *Survey of Old Testament Introduction.* 38.

363 Mater lectionis is a Latin phrase that translates to "mother of reading" in English. It refers to a pointing system used in Semitic languages like Hebrew, Arabic, and Syriac to indicate vowel sounds.

364 The reference to "a pre-Maccabean recension of the Hebrew Bible" is to historical period dating from the twenty-fourth century BCE (Genesis 27-29 appears to align with this historical period).

official copies in the temple archives) ...."[365] Professor Archer queries: "When did this hypothetical committee do its work? Some
have suggested the Council of Jamnia in A.D. 90, but this hardly
agrees with the evidence of texts like the Hebrew University Isaiah
Scroll, which corresponds almost letter for letter with MT and
yet dates from about 50 B.C.[366] A more likely supposition is that
the standardization of the consonantal text of the Old Testament
took place around 100 B.C.[367]

ARCHAELOGICAL TESTIMONY

In his, "Archaeological confirmation of the Old Testament," in
Carl F. Henry, Donald J. Wiseman observes that over 25,000 archaeological discoveries have been made in the Holy Land.[368] And
R.K. Harrison asserts that he has "yet to become acquainted with
any single archaeological find which by itself or in conjunction
with others specifically and categorically disproves the testimony
of the Old Testament."[369] Nelson Glueck, renown Jewish archae-

---

365 Gleason Archer Jr. A Survey of Old Testament Introduction. 43.

366 As astounding as Archer's statement regarding the amazing accuracy of the first Isaiah Scroll
(1QIsa) is, his comments concerning a second Isaiah Scroll discovered in Cave 1 (1QIsb) are
equally awe-striking: "Even though the two copies of Isaiah discovered in Qumran Cave 1 near
the Dead Sea in 1947 were a thousand years earlier than the oldest dated manuscript previously
known (A.D. 980), they proved to be word for word identical with our standard Hebrew Bible in
more than 95 percent of the text. The 5 percent of variation consisted chiefly of obvious slips of
the pen and variations in spelling. Even those Dead Sea fragments of Deuteronomy and Samuel
which point to a different text do not indicate any differences in doctrine or teaching. They do
not affect the message of revelation in the slightest." Josh McDowell. Evidence That Demands a
Verdict. 54.

367 Ibid. Dr. Archer develops footnote #7, in A Survey of the Old Testament Introduction (which is
matched to footnote #337, Dr. Archer's query above): "Moshe Greenberg comes to a somewhat
similar conclusion as a result of the Qumran data. He believes that the Jerusalem scribes began
systematically correcting and editing the text of the Old Testament as early as the third century
B.C., and that this project gained momentum under the Hasmonean (Maccabean) kings in the
second century. While the standardized text may not have prevailed until after the fall of Jerusalem, it is fair to say that 'the prevalence of the standard, not its creation, came after A.D. 70'
(Quoted in Burrows, MLDSS, p. 161. F. M. Cross in QHBT 186 suggests that the textus receptus
(of the MT) of the Pentateuch and the Former Prophets was the local text of the Babylonian
Jewish community established between the 4th and 2nd centuries B.C.)

368 Carl F. Henry, Revelation and the Bible (Waco, TX: Word, 1979), 301-302.

369 R.K. Harrison, Introduction to the Old Testament (Grand Rapids, MI: Eerdmans, 1969), 94.

ologist reinforces Harrison's assertion: "It may be stated categorically that no archaeological discovery has ever controverted a biblical reference."[370] Glueck continues in his observation of "the almost incredibly accurate historical memory of the Bible, and particularly so when it is fortified by archaeological fact."[371]

William F. Albright asserts: "There can be no doubt that archaeology has confirmed the substantial historicity of Old Testament tradition." Albright continues: "The excessive skepticism shown toward the Bible by important historical schools of the eighteenth and nineteenth centuries, certain phases of which still appear periodically, has been progressively discredited. Discovery after discovery has established the accuracy of innumerable details, and has brought increased recognition to the value of the Bible as a source of history."[372] Albright rests his case: "As critical study of the Bible is more and more influenced by the rich new material from the ancient Near East we shall see a steady rise in respect for the historical significance of now neglected or despised passages and details in the Old and New Testament."[373]

CLOSING ARGUMENT

"The perennial dilemma of man (corporate and personal)
as to the meaning of existence finds its resolution
in Christian revelation"

— John Warwick Montgomery.[374]

---

370 Nelson Glueck. Quoted in: Josh McDowell. *Evidence That Demands a Verdict*. San Bernardino, CA: Here's Life Publishers, INC. 1979 (rev.). 22.

371 Ibid. 65.

372 William F. Albright. *Christianity Today*. 18 January 1963.

373 See Josh McDowell, *Evidence That Demands A Verdict*, 68-73 for these and numerous other quotes and examples of specific archaeological discoveries that confirm both the testimony of the Old and New Testaments. The quotes ascribed to William F. Albright are from an interview with *Christianity Today*, 1963, 18.

374 John Warwick Montgomery. *Tractatus Logico-Theologicus*. 5.

Sir Frederick G. Kenyon, former director and principal librarian of the British Museum testifies to the full authority of Biblical Revelation in his, *The Story of the Bible*: "It is reassuring at the end to find that the general result of all these discoveries (of manuscripts) and all this study is to strengthen the proof of the authenticity of the Scriptures, and our conviction that we have in our hands, in substantial integrity, the veritable Word of God."[375]

---

375 Josh McDowell. *Evidence That Demands A Verdict.* 46.

BIBLIOGRAPHY

JOHN WARWICK MONTGOMERY

Montgomery, John Warwick. Editor. *Christianity for the Toughminded.* Minneapolis, MN: Bethany Fellowship. 1973.

_____. *Crisis In Lutheran Theology.* Rev. Ed. Two Vols. Minneapolis, MN: Bethany Fellowship. 1973.

_____. *Cross and Crucible.* Two Vols. The Netherlands. The Hague: Martinus Nijhoff. 1973.

_____. *Damned Through The Church.* Minneapolis, MN: Bethany Fellowship. 1970.

_____. *Debate On Situation Ethics.* Minneapolis, MN: Bethany Fellowship. 1972.

_____. "Defending the Gospel Through the Centuries," (Institute for Law & Gospel, Newport Beach, CA.; Cassette Album).

_____. *Demon Possession.* Minneapolis, MN: Bethany Fellowship. 1975.

_____. *Ecumenicity, Evangelicals, and Rome.* Grand Rapids, MI: Zondervan Publishing House. 1969.

_____. *Faith Founded On Fact.* Nashville, TN: Thomas Nelson Publishers. 1977.

_____. *History and Christianity.* Minneapolis, MN: Bethany Fellowship. 1970.

_____. *How Do We Know There Is A God?* Minneapolis, MN: Bethany Fellowship. 1974.

_____. *Human Rights & Human Dignity.* Grand Rapids, MI: Zondervan Publishing House. 1986.

_____. *In Defense of Martin Luther.* Milwaukee, WI: Northwestern Publishing House. 1970.

_____. *Jurisprudence: A Book Of Readings.* Strasbourg, France: International Scholarly Publishers. 1974.

_____. *Lawyer's Quest, Law & Gospel. A Study for Integrating Faith and Practice.* Reprint. Merrifield, VA: Christian Legal Society. 1986.

_____. *Myth, Allegory and Gospel*. Minneapolis, MN: Bethany Fellowship. 1974.

_____. *Principalities and Powers*. Minneapolis, MN: Bethany House Publishers, 1973.

_____. *Slaughter of the Innocents*. Westchester, IL: Cross-Good News Publishers. 1981.

_____, and Craig A. Parton. *The Art of Advocacy*. Minneapolis, MN: 1517 Academic. 2024.

_____. "The Cause and Cure of Sin," *Resource*, III. February 1962.

_____. *The Inerrant Word of God*. Minneapolis, MN: Bethany Fellowship. 1974.

_____. *The Law Above The Law*. Minneapolis, MN: Bethany Fellowship. 1975.

_____. *The Quest For The Ark*. Minneapolis, MN: Minneapolis, MN: Bethany Fellowship. 1972.

_____. *The Shape of the Past*. Rev. Ed. Minneapolis, MN: Bethany Fellowship. 1975.

_____. *The Shaping of America*. Minneapolis, MN: Bethany Fellowship. 1976.

_____. *The Suicide of Christian Theology*. Minneapolis, MN: Bethany Fellowship. 1970.

_____. *Theology: Good, Bad, and Mysterious*. Eugene, OR: WIPF & STOCK. 2020.

_____. *Tractatus Logico-Theologicus*. Eugene, OR: WIPF & STOCK. 2013.

_____. *Where is History Going?* Minneapolis, MN: Bethany House Publishers. 1969.

JOHN WARWICK MONTGOMERY: CONTRIBUTOR TO:

Evangelicals and Inerrancy. Ed. Ronald Youngblood. New York, NY: Thomas Nelson Publishers. 1984.

The Christian Idea of History. Donald C. Masters. Waterloo, Ontario: Waterloo Lutheran University. 1962.

The Meaning of the Death of God. Ed. Bernard Murchland. New York, NY: Random House Publishers. 1967.

The Philosophy of Gordon Clark. Ed. Ronald Nash. Phillipsburg, NJ: Presbyterian and Reformed Publishing. 1968.

The Rape of a Confessional Church. Ed. Dr. Reuben H. Redal and Dr. Paul G. Vigness. (Trial Transcript). 1980.

SECONDARY WORKS:

Aland, Kurt and Barbara. *The Text of the New Testament.* Grand Rapids, MI: Wm. B. Eerdmans. 1989.

Albright, William F. *Christianity Today* (Interview). January 18, 1963.

Althaus, Paul. *The Theology of Martin Luther.* Philadelphia, PA: Fortress Press. 1966.

Anderson, J.N.D. *Christianity: The Witness of History.* Downers Grove, IL: InterVarsity Press. 1970.

Anderson, Sir Norman. *The Evidence of the Resurrection.* Downers Grove, IL: InterVarsity Press. 1962.

Antonova, Stamenka E. *Barbarian or Greek? The Charge of Barbarism and Early Christian Apologetics.* Aristides. *Apology* 15.1. Series Ed. Robert J. Bast. Leiden (The Netherlands): Brill. 2019.

Archer, Gleason Jr. *Encyclopedia of Bible Difficulties.* Minneapolis, MN: Bethany House, 1982.

Augustine. *The City of God.* Ed. Whitney J. Oates. *Basic Writings of Saint Augustine.* Vol. Two. Grand Rapids, MI: Baker Book House. Reprinted: 1992.

_____. *Confessions.* Edited: Whitney J. Oates. *Basic Writings of Saint Augustine.* Vol. One. Grand Rapids, MI.: Baker Book House, Reprinted: 1992.

Bauer, Walter. *A Greek English Lexicon of the New Testament and Other Early Christian Literature.* Chicago, IL: The University of Chicago Press. Second Edition Revised and Augmented by: F. Wilbur Gingrich and Frederick W. Danker. 1979.

Beckwith, Francis. *Bahai.* Minneapolis, MN: Bethany Fellowship. 1985.

Bendall, Kent and Ferre', Frederick. *Exploring the Logic of Faith.* New York: Association Press, 1962.

Black, Henry Campbell. *Black's Law Dictionary, With Pronunciations.* Fifth Edition. St. Paul, MN: West Publishing CO. 1979.

Bruce, F.F. *The New Testament Documents: Are They Reliable?* Downers Grove, IL: InterVarsity Press. 1977.

Buswell, J. Oliver. *Being and Knowing.* Grand Rapids, MI: Zondervan. 1960.

Butterfield, Hebert. *Christianity and History.* London, UK. Collins Fontana Books. 1957.

Calvin, John. *Institutes Of The Christian Religion.* 4 Vols. Ed. John T. McNeill. Trans. Lewis Ford Battles. Philadelphia, PA: Westminster Press. 1960.

Carnell, Edward John. *An Introduction to Christian Apologetics.* Grand Rapids, MI: Wm. B. Eerdmans Publishing Co. 1948.

Colson, Charles. *Loving God.* Grand Rapids, MI: Zondervan. 1983.

Copleston, Fredrick S.J. *A History of Philosophy.* Volume V. "Hobbes to Hume." New Jersey: Paulist Press. 1959.

Crossan, John Dominic. *Who Killed Jesus? Exposing the Roots of Anti-Semitism in the Gospel Story of the Death of Jesus.* San Francisco, CA: Harper Collins. 1995.

Fee, Gordan. *The First Epistle To The Corinthians.* Grand Rapids, MI: Wm. B. Eerdmans Publishing Co. 1987.

Feinberg, Paul D. "History: Public or Private? A Defense of John Warwick Montgomery's Philosophy of History." *Christian Scholar's Review.* 1.4. Summer, 1971.

Fernandes, Phil. *The Fernandes Guide to Apologetic Methodologies.* Ottawa, Ontario, CAN: True Freedom Press, 2024.

Ferre' Frederick. "Mapping the Logic of Models in Science and Theology." *The Christian Scholar.* XLVI. Spring. 1963.

Flew, Antony. "Theology and Falsification." *New Essays in Philosophical Theology.* Editors: Antony Flew and Alasdair MacIntyre. London, UK: SCM Press. 1955.

Geisler, Norman and Nix, William. *A General Introduction to the Bible.* Chicago, IL: Moody Press. 1968.

_____. *Christian Apologetics.* Grand Rapids, MI: Baker Book House. 1976.

Gibson, Paul. *Bible Questions. Info.* "Why is the Masoretic Text Important? March 2 ND. 2019. https://biblequestions.info/2019/03/02/why-is-the-masoretic-text-important/. Downloaded: 02/18/2025.

Greenleaf, Simon. *Testimony of the Evangelists.* Newark, N.J: Soney & Sage. 1903.

Habermas, Gary R. & Licona, Michael R. *The Case for the Resurrection of Jesus.* Grand Rapids, MI: Kregel Publishing. 2004.

Hall, F.W. "Manuscript Authorities for the Text of the Chief Classical Writers." *A Companion to Classical Texts.* Oxford: Clarendon Press. 1913.

Harrison, R.K. *Introduction to the Old Testament.* Grand Rapids, MI: Eerdmans, 1969.

Henry, Carl F. *Revelation and the Bible.* Waco, TX: Word, 1979.

Hume, David. *An Enquiry Concerning Human Understanding.* "Of Miracles." Ed. Eric Steinberg. Indianapolis, IN.: Hackett Publishing Company. 1977.

Kasemann, Ernst. "Essays on New Testament Themes." *Studies in Biblical Theology.* No. 41. London: SCM Press, 1964.

Kenyon, Sir. Frederick G. *Handbook to the Textual Criticism of the New Testament.* 2nd Ed. London, UK: Macmillan. 1912.

_____. *The Bible and Archaeology.* New York, NY: Macmillan. 1925.

Kilner, John F. *Dignity and Destiny. Humanity in the Image of God.* Grand Rapids, MI: William B. Eerdmans, 2015.

Klausner, Joseph. *Jesus of Nazareth.* New York: Macmillan. 1925.

Künneth, Walter. "The Easter Message as the Essence of Theology." *Dialog.* (Spring, 1962).

Koukl, Gregory. "Augustine on Evil."

http://www.str.org/free/commentaries/apologetics/evil/augustine.htm. Downloaded: 05/13/2004.

Ladd, George. *I Believe in the Resurrection of Jesus.* Grand Rapids, MI: Wm. B. Eerdmans. 1975.

Lewis, C.S. *Mere Christianity.* The C.S. Lewis Signature Classics. San Francisco, CA: Harper One. 2017.

_____. *Miracles.* New York: Macmillan. 1960.

_____. *The Letters of C.S. Lewis to Arthur Greeves* (1914-1963). Edited by Walter Hooper. New York: Collier Macmillan, 1986.

Lewis, Gordon R. *Testing Christianity's Truth Claims.* Chicago, IL: Moody Press. 1976.

Mandelbaum, Maurice. *The Problem of Historical Knowledge*. New York: Harper & Row, 1967.

Martin, Walter R. *The Kingdom of the Cults*. Minneapolis, MN: Bethany House Publishers. Revised and expanded, 1985.

McCloskey, Patrick L. and Schoenberg, Ronald L. *Criminal Law Advocacy*. Vol. 5. New York: Mathew Bender. 1984.

McDowell, Josh. *Evidence That Demands a Verdict*. San Bernardino, CA: Here's Life Publishers, INC. 1979 (rev.).

McDowell, Josh & McDowell, Sean, *Evidence That Demands A Verdict: Life Changing Truth for a Skeptical World*. Thomas Nelson, 2017.

McDowell, Sean.

McGrath, Alister. *Luther's Theology of the Cross*. Oxford, UK: Basil Blackwell. 1985.

McRoberts, Kerry D. *A Letter from Christ, Apologetics in Cultural Transition*. Lanham, MD: University Press of America, INC. 2012.

_____. "The Holy Trinity." *Systematic Theology: A Pentecostal Perspective*. Ed. Stanley M. Horton. Springfield, MO: Logion Press. Rev. 1995.

_____. *The Woke Opiate. The Progressive Left's "Long March Through the Institutions."* Sydney, Aus.: Ark House Press. 2024.

Metzger, Bruce. *A Textual Commentary on the Greek New Testament*. Stuttgart, Germany. United Bible Society. 1971.

_____. *The History of New Testament Criticism*. Grand Rapids, MI: Wm. B. Eerdmans. 1963.

_____. *The Text of the New Testament*. New York, NY: Oxford University Press. 1964.

Moore, James R. "Science and Christianity." *Christianity for the Tough Minded*. Ed. John Warwick Montgomery. Minneapolis, MN: Bethany Fellowship, Inc. 1973.

Nash, Ronald. *Christian Faith and Understanding*. Grand Rapids, MI: Zondervan. 1984.

_____. "The Use and Abuse of History in Christian Apologetics." *Christian Scholar's Review*. Spring, 1971.

Packer, J.I. *God Has Spoken*. London: Hodder and Stoughton. 1979.

_____. *Knowing God*. Downers Grove, IL: InterVarsity Press. 1973.

Panneburg, Wolfhart. *Revelation as History*. New York, NY: Macmillan. 1968.

_____. *Faith and Reality.* Philadelphia, PA: Westminster. 1977.

Passmore, J.A. *Philosophical Analysis and History.* Ed. William H. Dray. New York, NY: Harper & Row. 1966.

Pitcher, George. *The Philosophy of Wittgenstein.* Englewood Cliffs: Prentice Hall. 1964.

Popper, Karl. *The Poverty of Historicism.* London, UK: Routledge and Kegan Paul. 1957.

Ramm, Bernard. *Protestant Christian Evidences.* Chicago, IL: Moody Press. 1953.

Ramsey, Ian. *Christian Discourse: Some Logical Explorations.* London, UK: Oxford, University Press. 1965.

Roberts, T.A. *History and Christian Apologetics.* London, UK: SPCK. 1960.

Robertson, A.T. *Introduction to the Textual Criticism of the New Testament.* Nashville, TN: Broadman Press. 1925.

_____. *Word Pictures in the New Testament.* Grand Rapids, MI: Baker Book House, 1931.

Robinson, James. "The Revelation of God in Jesus." *Theology as History.* Ed. James Robinson and John B. Cobb, Jr. New York, N.Y: Harper & Row. 1967.

Rosenbladt, Rod. "The Integrity of the Gospel Writers." *Christianity for the Tough-Minded.* Ed. John Warwick Montgomery. Minneapolis, MN: Bethany House Publishers. 1973.

Saunders, C. *Introduction to Research in English Literary History.* New York, N.Y: Macmillan. 1952.

Sherlock, Thomas. *The Tryal of the Witnesses of the Resurrection of Jesus.* London, UK: J. Roberts. 1729.

Sproul, R.C., Gerstner, John, Lindsley, Arthur. *Classical Apologetics.* Grand Rapids, MI: Zondervan. 1984.

_____. "The Case for Inerrancy: A Methodological Analysis." *God's Inerrant Word: An International Symposium on The Trustworthiness of Scripture.* Ed. John Warwick Montgomery.

Strauss, D.F. *Das Leben Jesu.* Darmstadt: Wissenschaftliche Buchesellschaft. 1835.

Toulmin, Stephen Edelston. *The Uses of Argument.* Cambridge, UK: The University Press. 1958.

Van Til, Cornelius. *A Survey of Christian Epistemology.* Den Dulk Foundation. 1969.

_____. *The Defense of the Faith.* Philadelphia, PA: Presbyterian and Reformed. 1955.

Warfield, B.B. *The Inspiration and Authority of the Bible.* Ed. Samuel G. Craig. Philadelphia: Presbyterian and Reformed Publishing Co. 1948.

Watkins, J.W.N. "Philosophy of History: Publication in English." *La Philosophie au milieu du vingtieme siècle.* Ed. Raymond Klibansky. 4 Vols. 2nd Ed. Firenze. 1961-62.

Watson, Philip S. *Let God Be God! An Interpretation of the Theology of Martin Luther.* London: Epworth Press. 1947

Wittgenstein, Ludwig. *Philosophical Investigations.* Trans. G.E.M. Anscombe, New York, NY: Macmillan Press. 1953.

_____. *Philosophical Review.* "Lecture on Ethics" (Part Two). Vol. 74. Number 1. Ed. Sage School of Philosophy, Cornell University. Ludwig Wittgenstein. "Lecture on Ethics." Delivered in November 1929 to the "Heretics Society." Cambridge University.

_____. *Tractatus Logico-Philosophicus.* Trans. D.F. Pears and B.F. McGuinness. London: Routledge. Reprint: 1994.

ABOUT THE AUTHOR

D R. KERRY "MAC" McROBERTS is a husband, father, grandfather, and above all, a covenant child of God by grace alone, through faith alone, in Christ alone. "Mac," (a nickname since serving in the United States Air Force), has served the purposes of the kingdom of God as a pastor, professor, apologist, author, academic dean, speaker, preacher, and as a guest lecturer and/or member of a world missions' cohort, on (besides North America) four continents: Europe, Asia, Latin America, and Africa.

Mac's senior pastoral career spans thirty-five years, and his teaching/academic career exceeds thirty years. Additionally, he has published seven books, coauthored three books and written several articles related to apologetics, social-ethics, theology, and missional congregations.

Mac has conducted numerous apologetics-oriented speaking events featuring debates on cults, the occult, and pagan spirituality, in the context of numerous Protestant Churches (e.g., Wesleyan, Episcopalian, Lutheran, Presbyterian, Nazarene, Baptist, Missionary Church USA, Mennonite Brethren, Assemblies of God). Mac's legal-historical apologetics career has been tested in postmodern, neo-pagan, socialist, and neo-Marxist cultures.

Mac has been quoted in over 1,200 scholarly papers (Academia.edu). He holds five academic degrees to include a D.Min. from Portland Seminary, Portland, OR., an MA in Systematic Theology, Regent College, Vancouver, B.C., Canada, and an MA in Apologetics, The Simon Greenleaf School of Law (now Trinity Law School), Santa Ana, CA. Mac is presently a Professor of Religion and Culture, Veritas International University, NM, and he is an adjunct professor (online) for Northwest University, WA. and North Central University, MN.

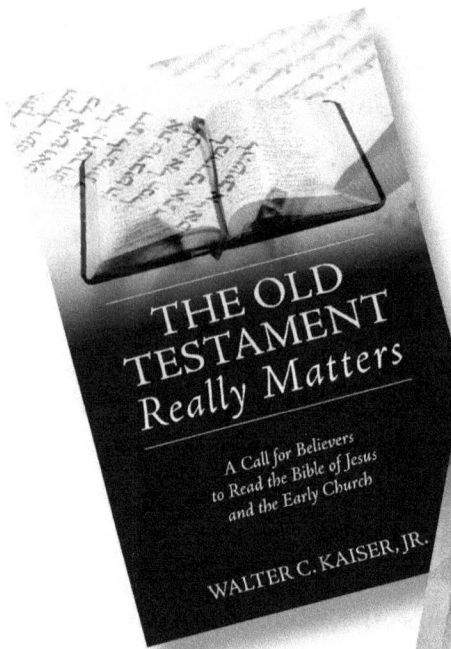